Addressing the Root of Jealousy

Why Some Might Hate You—Balancing Success and Relationships

Shawn Fisher

Table of Contents

Copyright

Foreword

My encouragement is for the reader to approach this work with an open heart, ready to explore the subtle yet profound ways in which jealousy can influence our lives. Jealousy is a universal emotion—familiar to us all—however understanding its roots and addressing it thoughtfully can transform our relationships, promote our spiritual growth, and enhance our outlook on life. It is my hope that this book serves as both a mirror and a guide: a mirror reflecting the ways jealousy may manifest within and around us, and a guide offering practical, Bible-based insights to foster peace, gratitude, and unity.

This work owes much to the guidance of a dear friend whose rigorous review and discerning feedback enriched every chapter. Her humility and desire to remain unnamed reflect the spirit of love and selflessness that this book seeks to inspire in its readers.

To all who read these pages, I encourage you to reflect deeply on the lessons within and incorporate them into your everyday interactions. My prayer is that you find hope in the practical tools for overcoming jealousy and cultivating stronger bonds with others. Above all, may you draw closer to Jehovah, the source of true contentment and joy.

Introduction

H ave you ever felt the weight of someone else's jealousy, even as you celebrated a hard-earned success? Perhaps it was a promotion you received at work, a goal you achieved after years of effort, or simply recognition for an accomplishment. At first, it's just a fleeting glance, a subtle shift in tone, or a half-hearted congratulations. But then, it deepens, coloring your interactions, as their envy begins to cast shadows over your joy. This book is for those moments— whether you find yourself the target of someone else's envy, leading to uncomfortable tension or even harsh persecution that has escalated into hatred, or whether you have allowed jealousy to take root in your own heart and are now struggling to overcome it.

Jealousy's Pervasiveness Across Life's Domains

Jealousy is an emotion we all encounter at some point, manifesting in different aspects of life. In personal relationships, it may arise as a subtle sting when comparing oneself to a friend or sibling who seems to have more opportunities, talents, or recognition. Within families, it can strain bonds when favoritism—real or perceived—leads to feelings of neglect or resentment. Professionally, jealousy often creeps into workplace dynamics. Even social settings are not immune; the rise of social media amplifies this emotion, as we're bombarded with curated highlights of others' lives, leaving us feeling inadequate or left behind.

The prevalence of jealousy in these diverse areas of life illustrates its far-reaching impact. Its effects can range from minor discomfort to severe damage to relationships, productivity, and personal well-being. This book acknowledges that while jealousy is a universal human experience, understanding and addressing it can lead to emotionally and spiritually transformative growth.

Reflecting on my own journey, I've often encountered situations where my efforts were misunderstood. Friends and family would marvel at the outcome but fail to see the countless hours of sacrifice, determination, and sleepless nights that made it possible. I vividly remember one instance: I had just received a promotion after years of hard work and consistently going above and beyond what was required. While I was deeply grateful for the recognition, I couldn't help but notice the strained smiles and distant behavior of those around me. "You're so lucky," one of them remarked, as if success had simply fallen effortlessly into my lap. One of them even went as far as organizing a petition to gather support against me being awarded the position. But behind their perception of "luck" was a reality of relentless work, doubts, and setbacks I had quietly overcome. It felt isolating, as if my achievements created a chasm between us, rather than a reason to celebrate together.

To be clear, every success, every ounce of strength to persevere, and every opportunity we encounter ultimately come from God. While hard work and effort are important, it is God's undeserved kindness and provision that makes anything possible. As James 1:17 (NWT*) reminds us, "*Every good gift and every perfect present is from above, coming down from the Father of the celestial lights.*" The abilities we possess, the endurance to keep going, and even the circumstances that align for success are not simply the result of "luck", chance, or personal effort, but gifts from the One who sustains us.

Why does success sometimes invite jealousy? Why do others so often see only the results and not the effort behind them? These questions have driven me to reflect deeply on the dynamics of envy and the way it intertwines with relationships. In this book, we'll explore these questions together, uncovering how jealousy is not just a reflection of others' insecurities but can also be an opportunity to cultivate empathy and strengthen bonds. Throughout this book, I draw upon various accounts from the Bible, where even faithful servants of God faced similar challenges. These examples provide valuable lessons to help us navigate such situations with grace and understanding.

A Path To Healing And Growth

Jealousy can feel overwhelming, leaving us trapped in cycles of comparison, resentment, and dissatisfaction. But what if instead of succumbing to its destructive effects, we could turn jealousy into an opportunity for growth, empathy, and deeper connections? This book is designed to guide you on a transformative journey from understanding the roots of jealousy to overcoming it with practical steps and spiritual insights.

From Trash To Treasure

Spectacle Island, located in Boston Harbor, offers a vivid illustration of transformation. Renowned for its abundance of sea glass, the island's beaches are scattered with colorful, weathered pieces of glass. What began as sharp, broken shards —discarded as trash—has been tumbled by waves, softened over time, and reshaped into something beautiful and unique. Each piece, once jagged and overlooked, becomes a treasured work of art, a testament to the relentless power of renewal. These remnants of the island's history as a landfill tell a powerful story: even the most discarded and broken things can be transformed into something of beauty.

This truth can be found in so many aspects of life, reminding us of the transformative power of time and persistence. Just as the ceaseless waves refine sea glass, our own emotional and spiritual healing can smooth the sharp edges of pain, envy, and strained relationships. With time, effort, and a willingness to change, even the most difficult moments of our lives—the struggles, mistakes, and heartbreaks—can be refined into something meaningful and beautiful.

The lesson of Spectacle Island extends beyond its shores. It reminds us that no part of our story is beyond repair or redemption. Even the painful, discarded, and broken pieces of our lives can be shaped into treasures through the process of healing.

Understanding the Roots of Jealousy

Before we can address jealousy, we must first recognize its origins. Why do we feel envious when others succeed? What triggers these feelings in ourselves or in others? By delving into the emotional and spiritual causes of jealousy, we uncover the insecurities, fears, and comparisons that fuel it. Through relatable examples and biblical accounts, you'll gain clarity on how jealousy begins and why it takes hold.

Recognizing Jealousy Within Ourselves

None of us are immune to this emotion, and it's important to identify when envy starts to take root in our hearts. Jealousy often begins subtly, feeding on feelings of inadequacy or unfairness. By understanding its triggers and acknowledging its presence, we can take proactive steps to correct these feelings before they grow into something more harmful. Through practical tools and guidance, this book will help you transform moments of jealousy—whether as the target or the source—into opportunities for personal growth.

Jealousy's corrosive effects extend beyond our relationships with others—it also damages our relationship with our Creator. When we allow envy to fester, we risk losing sight of Jehovah's purpose for us and the blessings He has given. The Bible reminds us that *"love is not jealous"* (1 Corinthians 13:4), underscoring that envy is incompatible with the love that should define our lives as His servants. Recognizing this danger is crucial, as maintaining a close relationship with God is foundational to our peace, happiness, and overall well-being.

Addressing External Manifestations

When others' jealousy targets us, it can feel isolating and painful. It may show up as subtle criticisms, strained relationships, or even outright hostility. In this book, we'll explore strategies for responding with grace and humility, helping to defuse tension while preserving your inner peace and spiritual focus. You'll learn how to navigate these situations without compromising your joy or your values.

Throughout this journey, you'll discover strategies for handling jealousy directed at you without losing sight of your own joy or alienating those who matter most. You'll learn how to gently shift the focus from envy to understanding and how to maintain humility in the face of admiration or resentment. We'll examine biblical examples and uncover practical insights on how to foster compassion and resilience when others view your success through a lens of comparison.

Confronting Internal Jealousy

Jealousy often begins within our own hearts, manifesting as feelings of inadequacy, frustration over perceived unfairness, or envy of a friend's achievements. This book provides tools for self-reflection and practical steps to address jealousy in ourselves. With honesty and vulnerability, we'll examine how to uproot envy, replacing it with gratitude, contentment, and trust in God's unique purpose for our lives.

Overcoming Jealousy Through Biblical Insights

The Bible provides profound wisdom on handling jealousy. From Joseph's endurance in the face of his brothers' envy to Cain's tragic failure to control his jealousy, Scripture offers timeless lessons on how to overcome this emotion. Throughout the book, these accounts will serve as powerful examples, showing how to transform jealousy into an opportunity for growth, faith, and stronger relationships.

It's essential to recognize that dealing with others' jealousy isn't just about protecting your emotional and spiritual well-being. It's about preserving relationships and fostering an environment where unity and mutual support thrive. Likewise, addressing jealousy within ourselves is vital for maintaining healthy, fulfilling relationships—with others and with God. Left unchecked, jealousy can quietly erode our connections, creating misunderstandings and resentment. By addressing it proactively, we can prevent these feelings from becoming barriers and instead transform them into opportunities for reconciliation and renewed faith.

Practical Personal Growth Strategies

This book aims to provide you with the knowledge and tools to navigate these challenges with integrity, grace, and compassion. By understanding the roots of jealousy, you'll be better prepared to defuse its impact and use those moments to reinforce your values of hard work, virtue, and humility. Together, we'll explore how to stay grounded in your self-worth and maintain meaningful relationships, even when others struggle to see beyond their own feelings.

Beyond understanding and reflection, this book equips you with actionable strategies for tackling jealousy in real life. From fostering empathy and encouraging collaboration to practicing mindfulness and cultivating gratitude, each chapter offers practical tools to help you rise above envy and build a life rooted in peace, humility, and spiritual strength. Integrating these strategies into your daily life will help you find freedom from the limitations jealousy imposes and empower you to embrace personal growth through gratitude, foster deeper connections with others, and draw closer to God.

Most importantly, you'll learn how to turn to God for help, trust in His wisdom, and find joy in His purpose for your life.

A Vision For The Future

Imagine a life where jealousy no longer holds power over you— where you celebrate others' successes wholeheartedly and embrace your unique path with confidence and contentment. Picture rising above the challenges of envy, both from others and within yourself, not with confusion or resentment, but with empathy and self-awareness.

See yourself engaging with others in ways that defuse tension and foster mutual respect. Instead of succumbing to rivalry or insecurity, you extend kindness and love, demonstrating that true success seeks to inspire, not overshadow. Jealousy loses its grip on you as your identity becomes firmly rooted in your inherent worth and unique blessings.

In this life, jealousy—whether from others or within yourself—no longer has the power to steal your joy. It becomes an opportunity to cultivate gratitude, deepen relationships, and grow spiritually. When envy arises, you meet it with understanding and grace, focusing on the blessings in your life and trusting in God's wisdom and timing.

Even in the face of envy, there is potential for connection, clarity, and healing. By choosing understanding over blame, self-reflection over division, and reliance on God over self-reliance, you can transform jealousy into a tool for deeper insight and stronger bonds. Let us embark on this journey together with hopeful hearts, uncovering the power of kindness, perseverance, and unwavering faith in God's guidance.

---

*All Bible scriptures referenced in this book are from the New World Translation (NWT), unless otherwise specified.

Chapter 1: Success

> *"Failure will never overtake me if my determination to succeed is strong enough."* —Og Mandino

Success often requires unwavering determination, the inner strength that doesn't falter in the face of adversity, obstacles, or criticism. Mandino's words remind us that the key to lasting success lies in our commitment to move forward, regardless of the challenges that arise. It's a call to resilience, encouraging us to give our best in every endeavor, and honoring the gifts and responsibilities entrusted to us. Through determination and focusing on our higher purpose, we can navigate achievement —embracing its positive aspects while rising above any negativity it may bring.

Success in every endeavor is a noble goal when it comes from a desire to give our best, and the Bible provides strong counsel on this point. The principle of doing one's best in every assignment is not just about personal achievement but about honoring God and reflecting His qualities in everything we do.

For example, Colossians 3:23 encourages: *"Whatever you are doing, work at it whole-souled as for Jehovah, and not for men."* This verse highlights the motivation behind our efforts. When we view our work as being done for God rather than just for human recognition, it gives us a higher purpose. It transforms every task, no matter how small or large, into an opportunity to glorify Him. Whether we are performing routine tasks or fulfilling a significant responsibility, working hard reflects the diligence and care God shows in His works.

The parable of the talents in Matthew 25:14-30 illustrates this principle. In this story, the master gives different amounts of talents (a type of money) to three servants. The two who worked diligently and doubled what was entrusted to them were commended as *"good and faithful"* servants (Matthew 25:21, 23). This shows that God values our efforts and our faithfulness in handling what He has given us—even in a secular sense. Whether we are given much or little, the key is how we use what we have to bring praise to Him.

Additionally, Ecclesiastes 9:10 says, , This further emphasizes that whatever task we undertake—whether big or small— should be done to the best of our ability. Our willingness to work hard and give our best reflects our gratitude for the skills, time, and opportunities God provides.

To illustrate, a gardener doesn't just plant seeds and walk away, hoping for success. He works diligently each day—watering, weeding, and nurturing the plants. His success is in the steady, faithful care he gives, knowing that the growth and outcome ultimately depend on God. Similarly, by doing our best in all our endeavors, we are like that gardener, knowing that our success is a result of our hard work paired with God's blessing.

Doing our best in every endeavor is, therefore, more than just a route to success; it is a biblical principle that honors God and demonstrates our faithfulness. By viewing our work as a way to glorify Jehovah and benefit others, we align ourselves with His purpose and reflect His qualities in every task. The result? Not only personal fulfillment when we succeed but also the assurance that our efforts contribute to something greater.

What Is Success?

What does it truly mean to be successful? The concept of success can vary widely depending on one's perspective, with definitions often shaped by personal values and cultural influences. In worldly terms, success is typically defined by the achievement of personal goals, the accumulation of wealth, or the gaining of recognition and status. It encompasses milestones such as career advancement, material possessions, or public admiration. In this context, success is measured by outward accomplishments and societal validation.

Conversely, the Bible presents a distinct understanding of success. In biblical terms, true success is rooted in a person's faithfulness to God and their commitment to living by His principles. Rather than focusing on external achievements, biblical success emphasizes qualities such as integrity, humility, and love. It involves honoring God through our actions, reflecting His character in everything we do, and fostering a deep relationship with Him. Ultimately, success in the Bible is about spiritual growth and the positive impact one has on others, rather than solely personal gain.

As you explore the material that follows, the term "success" will encompass both definitions. Whether referring to worldly accomplishments or spiritual fulfillment, the essence of success is ultimately intertwined with our motivations and the principles that guide our actions. Recognizing this duality allows us to appreciate the broader implications of success and encourages us to strive for excellence in every endeavor—honoring God while pursuing personal achievements.

Achieving True Success

Could there be a secret to success that many fail to recognize? In today's world, success is often measured by material achievements—wealth, status, or recognition. Yet, despite reaching these milestones, many still feel unfulfilled. This suggests that true success goes beyond external accomplishments. It involves something deeper, something that brings lasting satisfaction and purpose.

The Bible offers a different perspective, one that emphasizes inner qualities like wisdom, integrity, and faithfulness. It teaches that success is not just about reaching personal goals but about aligning one's life with values that lead to a closer relationship with God and long-term fulfillment. By following this guidance, individuals can experience a type of success that endures beyond temporary achievements.

Many people overlook this spiritual aspect of success because it doesn't always bring immediate rewards or applause. But those who embrace it find that their efforts, when guided by biblical principles, lead to a balanced and meaningful life. Success, from a biblical viewpoint, involves living in harmony with these principles—taking wise action, treating others with kindness, and staying true to Jehovah's values.

Ironically, living life in pursuit of true success, in alignment with Bible principles, often results in achieving what the world also recognizes as success. When a person is hardworking, honest, and compassionate—qualities highly esteemed in both spiritual and secular contexts—they tend to excel in their endeavors. Employers value integrity, diligence, and reliability, leading to promotions and career growth. Similarly, personal relationships flourish when people exhibit kindness and patience, which in turn brings a sense of social and emotional fulfillment.

Thus, while the focus of biblical success is not on material gain or social status, these often become welcome byproducts of living a life guided by sound biblical principles. A person who consistently acts with wisdom and fairness, for example, is likely to be trusted with greater responsibilities and opportunities. The individual who cultivates patience and humility is better equipped to handle the challenges and setbacks that are common in the workplace and in everyday life. This synergy between biblical principles and the worldly view of achievements shows that pursuing a higher standard brings inner peace and often results in tangible rewards that many seek in life.

Forgetting To Honor God

> "Who, then, is to have the things you stored up?" —Luke 12:20

The parable of the Rich Fool, found in Luke 12:16-21, powerfully illustrates the emptiness of equating success with the accumulation of wealth while neglecting a relationship with God. In this story, Jesus describes a wealthy man whose land produced an abundant harvest. Instead of expressing gratitude to God or considering how he could use his resources to benefit others, the man fixates on hoarding his wealth. He plans to build bigger storehouses to secure his riches and live a life of ease, viewing his material success as the ultimate measure of his worth. Yet God declares him a fool, saying, "This very night your life will be demanded of you," exposing the futility of placing ultimate trust in possessions. His wealth, now meaningless, is left behind.

This account underscores the fleeting nature of material success and the dangers of defining our value by what we accumulate. The Rich Fool's downfall wasn't his wealth itself but his obsession with it and his failure to acknowledge Jehovah as the source of his blessings and success. By contrast, focusing on spiritual priorities and gratitude reminds us of the temporary nature of material things and encourages us to use our resources wisely and generously. True success is not measured by wealth but by the richness of our relationship with God and our willingness to help others.

Applying the lessons of the Rich Fool's parable fosters humility and a balanced perspective on success. Instead of being consumed by the pursuit of wealth, we can focus on appreciating God's provisions—both spiritual and material—and using them to glorify Him. This mindset helps us avoid the anxiety, dissatisfaction, and emptiness that often accompany the relentless pursuit of material gain. Instead, it leads to the peace and fulfillment that come from trusting in God's care and aligning our resources with His purposes.

The parable challenges us to rethink what it means to be successful. Are we storing up riches for ourselves, chasing after fleeting material achievements? Or are we cultivating spiritual treasures by deepening our relationship with Jehovah and using our blessings to reflect His love and wisdom? True success comes not from accumulating wealth but from living a life that pleases God and benefits others, bringing lasting joy and eternal rewards.

Ultimately, the key distinction between worldly success and true success lies in one's motivation. While many pursue success for personal gain, those who follow biblical principles seek to reflect goodness, benefit others, and honor their Creator. For those who strive for true success, worldly markers such as wealth, recognition, and achievements are not the ultimate goals; rather, they are merely incidental to living wisely and righteously. By prioritizing spiritual values and aligning our actions with Bible principles, we find deep spiritual fulfillment and often attain accomplishments that others might view as conventional success.

How To Be Successful—God's Perspective

God instructed Joshua to meditate on His Word, promising that such meditation would lead to wise action and true success.

> "This book of the law should not depart from your mouth, and you must read it in an undertone day and night, in order to observe carefully all that is written in it; for then your way will be successful and then you will act wisely." — Joshua 1:8

God's instructions to Joshua serve as a powerful reminder that true success is deeply rooted in spiritual reflection and obedience. By telling Joshua to meditate on His Word "day and night," God emphasized the importance of consistent and deliberate focus on His principles. This was not merely about reading or memorizing laws, but about internalizing them—allowing God's guidance to shape thoughts, actions, and decisions. Joshua was assured that by doing so, he would be equipped for wise action and experience genuine success in his leadership role. His prosperity would come, not from his own strength or wisdom, but from his alignment with God's perfect guidance.

Similarly, Psalm 1:1-3 highlights the blessings of meditating on God's law:

> "Happy is the man who does not walk according to the advice of the wicked... But his delight is in the law of Jehovah, and he reads his law in an undertone day and night. He will be like a tree planted by streams of water, a tree that produces fruit in its season, the foliage of which does not wither. And everything he does will succeed." — Psalm 1:1-3

The passage from Psalm 1:1-3 further reinforces this concept by drawing a vivid illustration of the benefits of meditating on God's law. The man who delights in God's principles and reflects on them constantly is compared to a tree planted by streams of water. This imagery beautifully captures the idea of sustained growth and stability. Just as a tree with access to constant water thrives, producing fruit in its season and maintaining healthy foliage, similarly thrive those who meditate on God's Word. They are spiritually nourished, resilient, and successful in whatever they undertake. The tree's fruitfulness is a natural outcome of its constant connection to its life source, much like how spiritual prosperity results from regular, thoughtful meditation on God's teachings.

These verses highlight a timeless truth: success, from a biblical perspective, is not merely about reaching goals or acquiring material wealth. It's about cultivating a life that is in harmony with divine wisdom. When we meditate on God's Word and apply it in our lives, we are empowered to make wise decisions, avoid destructive paths, and experience the deep fulfillment that comes from living according to His will.

Moreover, the success that flows from following these principles is holistic. It encompasses spiritual, emotional, and even physical well-being. Just as the tree in Psalm 1 is vibrant and fruitful, so too are those who draw strength from God's wisdom. Their *"foliage does not wither"*—they remain steadfast even in challenging times. Their actions are guided by principles that lead to long-term success, not fleeting achievements and for this reason, verse three ends with the words: "*And everything he does will succeed.*" Consequently, success in the worldly sense often becomes a natural spin-off of pursuing true, biblical success.

In today's world, many people seek quick fixes or shortcuts to success, often following the *"advice of the wicked"* (Psalm 1:1) or the allure of questionable paths. However, the Bible consistently points out that real, lasting success comes from a divine source. By meditating on God's laws, we gain practical wisdom for everyday life and build a solid foundation that leads to enduring prosperity. This type of success builds the strength of our inner character, the quality of our relationships and brings us closer to our God.

Thus, both Joshua 1:8 and Psalm 1:1-3 emphasize that true success begins with a heart focused on Jehovah. As we prioritize His principles, we are assured that our way will be successful and that we will have the wisdom to navigate life's challenges effectively. Like the tree planted by streams of water, we too can experience the blessings of spiritual fruitfulness, stability, and success in all aspects of our lives.

Successful Men In The Bible

The Bible provides several examples of men who experienced true success because they followed God's guidance, as outlined in Joshua 1 and Psalm 1. These men were successful in their endeavors, and their lives were also marked by spiritual prosperity and favor from God. Throughout this book, we'll draw on the examples of Abel, Joseph, and David that exemplify this truth.

Abel

Abel is one of the earliest examples of someone who found favor in God's eyes through his faithfulness. His success was rooted in his devotion. Abel brought an offering to Jehovah that was the best of his flock, an indication that he understood the importance of giving God his best. Abel's success was not measured by material gain or public recognition but by his faith and obedience to God's standards.

Abel's legacy lives on as the earliest model of true spiritual success. His faith is mentioned in Hebrews 11:4, demonstrating that God regarded Abel's offering as righteous because it reflected a heart focused on pleasing God.

Joseph

Joseph's life is a powerful example of how following God's principles leads to both spiritual and material success. Despite being sold into slavery and later wrongfully imprisoned, Joseph remained faithful to God in all circumstances. His focus on God's principles enabled him to be successful. Genesis 39:2-3 tells us that *"Jehovah was with Joseph,"* and as a result, everything he did prospered.

Joseph's steadfast reliance on God's guidance allowed him to rise to a position of great authority in Egypt, where he ultimately saved many lives, including those of his own family, during a time of famine. His success was in his rise to power and in his unwavering integrity and faithfulness. He rejected temptation, remained humble, and attributed his success to God's blessing.

David

David, like Abel and Joseph, experienced success because of his faithfulness to God. Throughout his early life, David demonstrated reliance on God's support, whether as a shepherd boy defending his flock or as a warrior defeating Goliath. His victories were not solely based on his skill or courage, but *"David was successful in all his ways, [because] Jehovah was with him."* (1 Samuel 18:14)

David's devotion to meditating on and applying God's law, as reflected in many of his psalms, contributed to his success as a king and being a man after God's own heart. Even though David faced challenges and made mistakes, his overall pattern of seeking God's guidance ensured that his reign was marked by divine favor and blessing.

Spiritual Foundations Of Real Success

In the case of Joseph and David, their success was not the result of worldly ambition. They meditated on and applied God's laws, making decisions based on His principles rather than human wisdom. While their paths were not free of challenges, their commitment to God led to spiritual success, and this also translated into worldly success. Joseph rose to a high position in Egypt and preserved his family; David became Israel's greatest king, known for his heart that pursued God.

These men exemplify that true success, as defined by the Bible, comes from faithfulness to God, meditation on His Word, and adherence to His guidance. Just as Joshua 1 and Psalm 1 promise, those who follow God's laws are like trees planted by streams of water—resilient, fruitful, and prosperous in all that they do. Through their lives, we see that spiritual success often brings blessings that can be evident in material terms, as God's favor brings both spiritual and practical prosperity.

There is, therefore, a clear caution: the pursuit of worldly success must always be secondary to a life centered on God. Solomon's life serves as a powerful example of this principle. In Ecclesiastes 12:13, he reflects on the lessons of his unparalleled experiences, stating, *"The conclusion of the matter, everything having been heard, is: Fear the true God and keep His commandments, for this is the whole obligation of man."* Despite achieving immense wealth, wisdom, and fame, Solomon came to realize that when pursuits are disconnected from God, they ultimately amount to *"vanity"* and striving after the wind (Ecclesiastes 1:14). His life reminds us that true success is defined not by what we achieve materially, but by how we align our lives with God's purpose.

Solomon's journey highlights the emptiness of pursuing success solely for personal gain. He had the means to explore every form of worldly achievement, from grand architectural projects and immense riches to indulgence in pleasures and intellectual pursuits. Yet, without God's guidance, these endeavors left him unfulfilled. When Solomon says, *"everything having been heard,"* he is essentially declaring, *"I've experienced it all—success, failure, excess, and moderation—and I've learned that apart from Jehovah, none of it has real meaning or lasting satisfaction."* His insight reminds us that true success is not found in wealth, fame, or human accomplishments, but in living a life devoted to God.

This caution is particularly relevant in a world that often equates success with material gain or personal recognition. Solomon's wisdom helps us understand that when success is pursued at the expense of spiritual priorities, it leads to frustration and spiritual emptiness. Jesus echoed this principle in Matthew 6:33, saying:

> *"Keep on, then, seeking first the Kingdom and His righteousness, and all these other things will be added to you."* —Matthew 6:33

This verse reinforces that God provides for our needs when we place spiritual pursuits above worldly ambitions.

Those who follow God's laws, like Abel, Joseph, and David, demonstrate that true success comes from aligning our lives with His will. Their lives show that spiritual prosperity often results in blessings that extend into practical areas as well. However, the examples of Solomon and others remind us that these blessings are not the primary goal—they are byproducts of faithfulness to God.

Ultimately, Solomon's conclusion encourages us to focus on what truly matters. While worldly success may bring temporary satisfaction, only a life lived in harmony with Jehovah's principles provides lasting happiness and purpose. This balance, which is explored further in Chapter 5, helps us approach success with humility, gratitude, and a heart fully devoted to God's will.

Chapter 2: Jealousy—Drawn To Success

Abel, Joseph, and David each demonstrate that true success comes from a deep, ongoing relationship with God. Their faithfulness to God brought them both spiritual prosperity and tangible blessings. Yet, their experiences reveal an important insight. When Jehovah blesses someone, success can attract jealousy. Jealousy, from seeing someone else's good fortune, can drive people to harmful actions, and these actions often have lasting effects.

In modern times, the tangible rewards of success are frequently tied to money, which acts as the enabler of material gain. When people become jealous of another's success, their focus often shifts from the achievements themselves to the material rewards that accompany it. Instead of admiring or aspiring to emulate the qualities that led to success, they begin to covet the perceived advantages. This fixation on material benefits can foster an unhealthy love for money, as it becomes a symbol of what they feel they lack or desire. Over time, this love for money grows, influencing attitudes and actions in deeply harmful ways.

Imagine a man named John who had lived in a neighborhood for years, quietly working a steady job. After receiving a significant promotion, John's life seemed to transform. He bought a new car, a boat, and began renovating his home. His neighbor, Mark, started to feel envious, questioning why John deserved such success. As his jealousy grew, Mark began spreading rumors about John, insinuating that he must have cheated his way to the top. This strained their relationship and tainted John's reputation in the neighborhood. Scenarios like these play out in many neighborhoods today and illustrate how jealousy, fueled by material comparisons, can escalate into harmful behaviors that damage relationships within the community.

In this context, jealousy and materialism become intertwined, fueling thoughts and behaviors that can result in negative actions. This connection helps us understand why the Bible declares, (1 Timothy 6:10). Jealousy often serves as the seed, but it is sometimes the unchecked desire for material gain—and the money that facilitates it—that takes root, ultimately leading individuals down a path of harm, both to themselves and to others.

While the love of money is the root of all evil, jealousy often plants the initial seed from which such evil grows. Long before wealth or material desires became a snare, this insidious seed took root in the heart of a being so wretched that it envied the glory and position of another. That envy sprouted, growing into lies and deceit, and ultimately culminated in the first act of murder. This dynamic has been evident since ancient times and reveals jealousy's tragic potential. Over the millennia, jealousy's roots have twisted through human history, producing the bitter fruits of greed, hatred, and violence—fruits that humanity continues to reap to this day.

Given the destructive nature of jealousy, one might naturally wonder, "If jealousy is such a harmful trait, why does the Bible describe Jehovah as a 'jealous' God?" This is a valid question, especially given that human jealousy, as we have observed through our own experiences, often gives rise to negative emotions and actions. By definition, jealousy is an intense feeling that arises when someone feels threatened or resentful about another's success, qualities, or possessions. It is typically marked by insecurity, comparison, and envy, which can drive harmful thoughts or behaviors toward the perceived rival. Human jealousy often stems from selfishness or a sense of inadequacy, leading to bitterness, resentment, and even destructive actions. However, God's jealousy is entirely different in nature and purpose.

Different Types Of Jealousy

When the Bible refers to God as being *jealous*," it describes a very different kind of jealousy—based in His deep love and righteous desire for our exclusive devotion, not insecurity or rivalry. Research material* explains that the Hebrew word for God's "jealousy" may be translated as "toleration of no rivalry" toward Him, reflecting His rightful claim on His people's devotion. For this reason, Exodus 34:14 says,

> *"For thou shalt worship no other god, for Jehovah, whose name is Jealous, is a jealous God."* —Exodus 34:14 (ASV)

This form of jealousy is not about envying someone else's position or possessions but about God's rightful expectation of loyalty from those who serve Him. As the Creator, He has a unique, loving relationship with His people, and His "jealousy" reflects His concern for their well-being.

Unlike human jealousy, which is rooted in insecurity and selfishness, God's jealousy is a reflection of His unwavering commitment to His people. It is not born out of envy or fear but out of a deep desire to protect the purity of worship and the relationship He has with His servants. God's divine jealousy is an expression of His loyalty and care, ensuring that His people remain faithful and avoid the harm that comes from turning away from Him. Thus, God's jealousy is not a flaw or a vice, but rather a testament to His steadfast love and justice.

For instance, when the Israelites worshiped the golden calf, God's righteous jealousy prompted Him to act decisively, both to discipline those who had turned away and to protect the purity of His worship (Exodus 32:9-10). Allowing them to continue in idolatry would have led to spiritual ruin, distancing them from Jehovah and opening the door to harmful practices such as child sacrifice, immorality in false worship, and reliance on powerless idols. These actions would harm their spiritual relationship with God and lead to societal corruption and personal suffering. This example underscores how His jealousy safeguards His people's relationship with Him, highlighting His unwavering commitment to their spiritual welfare.

God's jealousy is, like that within a marriage, protective and honorable, rather than possessive. Unlike human jealousy, which often harms relationships, God's jealousy arises from love and is directed toward keeping us from things that could harm us spiritually. Just as a parent might be "jealous" over the safety and loyalty of their child—deeply concerned if they were to follow harmful influences—God's jealousy is focused on our spiritual welfare. He knows that straying from Him would lead to needless suffering. His jealousy is an expression of His desire to protect us.

In contrast, human jealousy is rooted in selfishness, insecurity, and lack of trust in God. At its core, it reflects a self-centered desire to control outcomes instead of trusting that God provides for our true needs. Instead of resting in the assurance that He knows what is best for us and will provide in His perfect time, human jealousy focuses on what we perceive we are lacking at present. This form of jealousy can distort our perspective and damage relationships, pushing us to resent or even harm those we feel threatened by.

Jehovah's jealousy, however, is pure and righteous, aimed at preserving the loving relationship He desires to have with us. This form of jealousy comes from a place of strength, justice, and unwavering love. It serves as a reminder that He values our devotion and wants us to experience the benefits of a close relationship with Him. While jealousy in humans often leads to destructive thoughts and actions, God's jealousy is a reminder of His deep love and commitment, inviting us to draw close to Him and stay loyal for our ultimate good.

Throughout this book, the term "jealousy" specifically refers to the human form of jealousy—marked by insecurity, envy, and of rivalry—not the righteous, protective jealousy displayed by our Creator. Therefore, as you read, please keep in mind that any references to jealousy are focused on the human experience of jealousy and its negative impact on individuals and relationships.

Jealousy's Unique And Consuming Nature

Jealousy can sometimes be mistaken for hate; however, it is far more insidious. Like a small, seemingly harmless crack in the foundation of a house, jealousy often goes unnoticed at first. It begins as a barely visible hairline fracture that doesn't disrupt daily life. But if left unaddressed, that crack quietly spreads, weakening the structure until one day, without warning, the house collapses. Jealousy works in much the same way. It starts as a faint whisper in our hearts—admiration mingled with a subtle longing. Over time, however, it grows silently and insidiously, undermining our inner peace and relationships until its destructive force becomes impossible to ignore. Just as a homeowner must repair even the smallest crack to protect their home, we must confront jealousy early to prevent it from corroding the foundation of our lives.

Unlike hate, which is usually directed outwardly and can be addressed more directly, jealousy often begins as a subtle, inward feeling that quietly grows. It tends to be more personal, frequently going unrecognized by the person harboring it. Initially, jealousy might seem like harmless admiration of someone else's success, appearance, or relationships. But over time, it subtly twists into resentment, often without the person even realizing how deeply it has taken root.

Imagine a young artist named Leah who often admired her best friend Mia's success. Mia's paintings were frequently featured in exhibitions, and she seemed to have an effortless talent that Leah couldn't help but admire. At first, Leah's admiration motivated her—she spent more time practicing her art, hoping to improve. But as Mia's accolades grew, Leah began to notice a subtle shift in her feelings. She started comparing every brushstroke of her work to Mia's, criticizing her own efforts harshly.

One day, while scrolling through social media, Leah saw a post celebrating Mia's latest award. Instead of feeling happy for her friend, Leah felt a pang of resentment. "Why does she get all the recognition?" she thought. Leah didn't realize it, but what started as innocent admiration had quietly turned into jealousy. This change wasn't obvious to anyone else—not even to Leah at first—but it began to affect their friendship. Leah withdrew, feeling bitter and insecure, all because she hadn't addressed the growing "crack" in her heart.

It is not clear when exactly this shift from admiration to resentment occurs. One moment, the person might genuinely appreciate someone else's success or qualities, even feeling inspired by them. But gradually, without conscious awareness, those feelings begin to sour. The admiration that once felt uplifting starts to sting as comparisons creep in, and a feeling of inadequacy or injustice takes hold. This leaves the person harboring jealousy feeling betrayed—not by others, but by her own emotions. This inner turmoil doesn't remain confined to the individual; it inevitably spills over, straining relationships as jealousy clouds perceptions and influences interactions with others.

This self-betrayal intensifies the feeling of jealousy because it creates an internal conflict. On the one hand, the individual may want to celebrate or emulate the person they initially admired; on the other, they feel a growing bitterness they cannot fully explain or control. This inner turmoil can lead to shame or guilt, as the person struggles with feelings he may know are irrational but cannot seem to overcome. Over time, this cycle of admiration, resentment, and self-reproach can deepen the emotional wound, making jealousy even more insidious and damaging to both the individual and his relationships.

Have you ever felt torn between admiration and resentment for someone else's achievements? Envy is particularly destructive because it clings to us in a way other emotions may not. Rooted in feelings of inadequacy or insecurity, jealousy acts like a mirror that reflects our desires and our perceived shortcomings. Every time we see or think of someone who possesses what we covet, the feeling intensifies, creating a relentless cycle of discontent. As Ecclesiastes 4:4 observes, "I have seen how much effort and skillful work spring from rivalry between people." This verse captures how jealousy can transform admiration into rivalry, turning our focus from appreciation to comparison.

Unlike other negative emotions that may diminish over time, jealousy often festers and simmers, feeding on our insecurities and driving constant comparison. Where hate might lead us to avoid someone, jealousy has the opposite effect; it keeps us fixated on the person we envy, intensifying our dissatisfaction and eroding our self-worth. Proverbs 14:30 reflects on this internal damage, saying, "A calm heart gives life to the body, but jealousy is rottenness to the bones." The corrosive nature of jealousy strips us of inner peace, consuming us from within.

Jealousy thus differs from hate in its deeply personal nature. While hate can be directed toward external factors, jealousy often feels like a reflection of our own insecurities, targeting our self-worth. Rather than an outward opposition, it creates a feeling of inadequacy within, making it harder to manage or dismiss. This is why jealousy is so damaging: it leaves us feeling betrayed, diminishes both our perception of others and of ourselves, and undermines our inner stability.

In addition, jealousy can drive us to negative actions much faster than hate due to its all-consuming nature. While hate might lead to avoidance, jealousy often compels us to seek relief from inner turmoil. The sting of jealousy is relentless, constantly reminding its host of perceived shortcomings or lack, offering no respite. This unrelenting mental and emotional agitation drives individuals to pursue relief, often through actions aimed at regaining inner peace—actions that can ultimately harm both themselves and others.

James 3:16 warns, "For wherever there are jealousy and contentiousness, there will also be disorder and every vile thing." This scripture underscores the chaos that jealousy brings into our lives, creating fertile ground for destructive behavior. How can we break free from jealousy's grip and rediscover peace? By recognizing the consuming and compulsive nature of jealousy, we can become more aware of its presence and take intentional steps to guard against its harmful influence, thereby preserving both our inner peace and our relationships.

Jealousy And Self-Worth

> "No one can make you feel inferior without your consent."
> —Eleanor Roosevelt

Roosevelt's words remind us of the power we hold over our own self-worth. Jealousy and comparison often lure us into surrendering that power. When we compare ourselves to others, we're not just assessing their achievements; we're questioning our own value. This act of comparison slowly erodes our happiness, shifting our focus from what we have to what we lack. Jealousy amplifies this effect, convincing us that someone else's success somehow reduces our own, leaving us feeling diminished. This mindset traps us in a cycle of dissatisfaction, making it nearly impossible to appreciate our own strengths and accomplishments. As we continue to measure ourselves against others, joy is stolen, and our sense of identity becomes entangled in a constant feeling of inadequacy.

Jealousy, thus, doesn't just focus on what others possess; it strikes at our self-worth. When we feel envious, we compare our value, abilities, or possessions to someone else's. This creates a harmful cycle of insecurity that becomes self-perpetuating. As we compare ourselves, we begin to believe that the successes or qualities of others somehow diminish our own. Jealousy, then, feeds on our insecurities and makes us feel as if we are constantly falling short, diminishing our self-esteem.

Jealousy thrives in a world that constantly encourages comparison. From early childhood, individuals are often measured against others through academic performance, athletic achievements, or social milestones. As adults, this culture of comparison evolves but does not disappear; it is reinforced by societal expectations and amplified by modern platforms like social media.

Social media, in particular, has created a unique environment where people's successes, beauty, and lifestyles are curated into seemingly perfect snapshots. These filtered realities can make it appear as though others are effortlessly achieving the very things we struggle to attain, whether they are career advancement, financial stability, relationships, or even physical appearance. The more we scroll, the more we compare, and the more we feel inadequate.

Furthermore, cultural narratives often equate self-worth with productivity, possessions, or outward success. Messages like "You're only as good as your latest achievement" or "More is better" encourage a mindset in which contentment feels like settling, and the bar for personal satisfaction is always set higher. This societal pressure exacerbates feelings of inadequacy and makes it difficult to appreciate our own unique journeys and blessings.

This connection between jealousy and self-identity can lead us to feel less capable, less valuable, or, worst of all, less lovable. It forces us to question why we lack what others seem to possess so easily, deepening our dissatisfaction with ourselves. Jealousy brings the struggle inward, making us feel inadequate and powerless. As jealousy shapes our self-perception, we may even begin to act in ways that reinforce those feelings, turning us into our own worst critics.

Recognizing these external influences is key to understanding why the cycle of comparison and jealousy is so persistent. When we see how societal norms and curated realities fuel this dynamic, we can begin to challenge those narratives and focus on what truly brings lasting joy and fulfillment.

As we have seen, jealousy can drive us to take drastic, sometimes irrational, actions to try and "fix" what we perceive as lacking. It can lead us to sabotage relationships, compromise our values, or even harm others to elevate ourselves. This pursuit of what we don't have—or our desire to bring others down—clouds our judgment and often distances us from our true potential. By making us feel perpetually incomplete, jealousy leaves us in a state of constant dissatisfaction. James 4:2 illustrates this drive, stating, "*You desire, and yet you do not have. You go on murdering and coveting, and yet you are not able to obtain. You go on fighting and waging war.*"

Ultimately, jealousy is not just about wanting what others possess—it is about losing sight of our own inherent value, eroding the foundation of self-identity with a persistent whisper that we are not enough. In the end, this relentless feeling undermines our joy, tainting our perspective and disconnecting us from the fulfillment that comes from truly appreciating who we are.

Healing From Jealousy's Wounds

Whether through the written record of the Bible or personal experience, the consequences of jealousy underscore a vital truth: when left unchecked, it leads to disorder and paves the way for harmful actions. It warps judgment, blinds us to reality, and fosters a spirit of rivalry and contention. This destructive emotion creates an environment of chaos, feeding a narrative of scarcity and competition that very often doesn't exist. The Bible warns us of this danger in Proverbs 27:4 which captures this destructive potential, saying,

> *"There is the cruelty of rage and the flood of anger, but who can withstand jealousy?"* —Proverbs 27:4

What makes jealousy so uniquely dangerous is its subtle yet pervasive nature. Unlike hate, anger, or frustration, which may flare up and then dissipate over time, jealousy tends to linger, festering beneath the surface. It is a quiet, insidious emotion that, if allowed to grow, can consume a person entirely. Those who fall prey to jealousy often find it difficult to escape its grip, as it convinces them that happiness and self-worth are always just out of reach, contingent upon possessing what others have. It can drive people to betray, harm, and even take the lives of those closest to them, ultimately leading to devastation. Proverbs 6:34-35 speaks to this, saying,

> *"For jealousy makes a husband furious; He will show no compassion when he takes revenge. He will accept no compensation; He will not be appeased, no matter how large you make the gift."* —Proverbs 6:34-35

This chapter serves as a sobering reminder of the dangers of jealousy. However, there is hope. While jealousy is a powerful emotion, it is not insurmountable. The Bible reassures us that, with God's guidance and our determined effort, we can break free from its grip and experience lasting peace. The strategies provided in this book are designed to assist you on that journey.

> *"It's in the process of embracing our imperfections that we find our true beauty."* —Unknown

The preceding quote aligns well with the Japanese aesthetic of *wabi-sabi*, which finds beauty not in perfection, but in imperfection, impermanence, and incompleteness. It celebrates the natural wear and weathering of life, valuing the cracks, scratches, and irregularities that tell a story of resilience and authenticity. Just as a kintsugi artisan mends broken pottery with gold, highlighting its fractures rather than hiding them, *wabi-sabi* teaches us that our imperfections are not flaws to be masked but unique marks of our journey, giving us depth and character.

This philosophy reminds us that life's true beauty emerges when we embrace the process of transformation, even when it feels messy or broken. It is in the acceptance of life's imperfections and the honoring of its natural flow that we discover our true potential. Through the lens of *wabi-sabi*, what is damaged or incomplete becomes not less, but more valuable—more meaningful for its journey through time.

The concept of *wabi-sabi*—finding beauty in imperfection and transience—offers a parallel lesson. Like broken pottery mended with gold, our struggles with jealousy can lead to profound personal growth. Embracing our flaws, rather than masking them, strengthens our humility and fosters authentic relationships. When jealousy arises, we can choose to grow, turning mistakes into opportunities to become more generous, grateful, and resilient.

---

*Watch Tower Bible and Tract Society of Pennsylvania (1995) *The Bible's Practical Wisdom—A Guide to Happiness.* Watchtower Online Library. Available at: https://wol.jw.org/en/wol/d/r1/lp-e/1995683#h=4 (Accessed: 29 November 2024).

Chapter 3: Jealousy Turns Diabolical

The ripple effects of jealousy are devastating. Relationships are destroyed, trust is eroded, and spiritual peace is replaced by turmoil. The biblical accounts of Cain, Joseph's brothers, and King Saul show that jealousy does more than harm others—it corrodes the very hearts of those who harbor it, driving them to extreme and destructive actions. As we examine their experiences, we see how jealousy distorts perception, transforming friends into enemies, family into rivals, and blessings into sources of bitterness.

These accounts serve as powerful warnings about the dangers of letting jealousy take root in our hearts. They remind us of the importance of confronting envy early, turning to God for help, and striving to cultivate love and humility instead. Only then can we safeguard our relationships, our peace of mind, and our standing with our Creator.

Jealousy Was Behind The First Murder

"Am I my brother's keeper?" —Genesis 4:9 (ASV)

The story of Cain and Abel is as old as time itself and illustrates the destructive path that jealousy can carve through human relationships. In their story, jealousy, as the first negative emotion ever displayed between humans, grew into something far more sinister, ultimately leading to a tragic act that would forever stain Cain's life and mark the beginning of jealousy's destructive legacy on humanity.

Abel pleased God and his success came through his righteous offering, which was accepted because it came from a heart of genuine faith and devotion. However, Abel's faithfulness stirred jealousy in his brother, Cain. Rather than viewing Abel's offering as an example to aspire to and using Abel's success as an opportunity to reflect on his own offering, Cain allowed his envy to fester and saw his brother's success as a threat to his own standing with Jehovah. His jealousy led to an act so hideous that it forever marked mankind: the first murder in human history. This was no ordinary crime, as it was driven not by self-defense or survival but by unchecked jealousy. Cain's crime was especially grievous because it was an attack on his own brother—a sibling he should have loved and protected. Instead, jealousy consumed him to the extent that he lured Abel into a field and mercilessly took his life.

The gravity of Cain's offense lies in the physical act of murder and in the deeper betrayal of family bonds and the rejection of God's guidance. Cain had received a direct warning from God to control his emotions, as revealed in Genesis 4:7, but he ignored this counsel. Instead, he allowed sin to "crouch at the door" of his heart, ultimately permitting it to overpower him. The imagery of "sin crouching at the door" vividly portrays sin as a predatory force, akin to a wild animal lying in wait, ready to pounce on its prey. This metaphor highlights sin's persistent nature and its active intent to exploit moments of human vulnerability—especially in the context of Cain's jealousy. Cain's resentment over Abel's acceptance by God became the opening through which sin began its assault, skewing his perception and hardening his heart. This underscores the need for personal accountability, vigilance, and self-awareness to resist destructive impulses.

After committing the heinous act of murdering his brother, Cain's response to God's inquiry further revealed the depth of his spiritual downfall. When God asked him, "Where is your brother Abel?" Cain infamously replied, "I do not know. Am I my brother's keeper?" (Genesis 4:9). This response was not only a blatant lie, but it also demonstrated a shocking lack of remorse or accountability for his actions. His words reveal a cold indifference to the life he had just taken, along with a refusal to acknowledge his responsibility.

Cain's response was a deflection of responsibility that resonates with modern attitudes of evasion and blame-shifting. For example, in workplace settings, individuals may shift accountability for failures onto colleagues to protect their own interests, or, in familial disputes, one might deflect guilt by pointing fingers at others. Such behaviors highlight how jealousy or guilt can undermine personal responsibility, mirroring Cain's own avoidance of ownership for his actions.

Cain's lie adds another layer of gravity to his crime. Lying, in itself, is a serious offense, but to lie directly to Jehovah—the One who sees and knows all—is particularly audacious. His attempt to deceive God demonstrates how jealousy and sin can blind a person, leading him to act irrationally, as though he could hide his wrongdoing from the Almighty. In his reply to God, he suggested that he had no obligation to look after his brother's well-being. His response is both callous and deeply ironic because, as Abel's older brother, Cain certainly had a responsibility to care for and protect him, rather than to harm him.

Moreover, Cain's question reflects a hardened heart, one that refused to acknowledge the seriousness of his sin. His indifference to Abel's death illustrates how far jealousy and hatred had taken root in his heart. Cain had moved beyond mere envy or anger; he had entered a state of denial and defiance, choosing to harm his brother and dismiss any responsibility for the life he had taken. His refusal to confess or repent shows how jealousy, when left unchecked, can lead to a downward spiral of increasingly grievous offenses.

This moment in the narrative marks a significant turning point in human history. Not only had the first murder been committed, but Cain's lie and his flippant attitude toward Abel's death revealed the far-reaching impact of jealousy. What began as jealousy—a feeling that many might dismiss as harmless—had escalated into murder and then compounded into deception and denial before God. Cain's question, inquiring of God whether he was his brother's keeper, speaks volumes about his inner state. It shows that he rejected his familial duty to Abel and his spiritual duty to God. In contrast to Abel, who offered a pleasing sacrifice from a heart of faith, Cain's actions revealed a heart that had distanced itself from God and was now willing to defy Him openly.

Cain's rejection of his duties mirrors broader themes of accountability and responsibility that resonate throughout human relationships. By denying his obligation to Abel, Cain symbolizes the breakdown of communal care and the rejection of a divine mandate to protect and nurture one another. This act highlights a universal moral failure in which self-interest overrides collective responsibility. In contemporary settings, we see echoes of this in societal indifference or even harm toward vulnerable individuals, illustrating that the abdication of responsibility can lead to relational fractures and communal instability.

This episode highlights the insidious nature of jealousy. It often begins subtly but can rapidly escalate into far more serious transgressions. Rather than humbling himself, admitting his sin, and seeking forgiveness, Cain chose to deflect, deny, and distance himself from accountability. His attempt to shift blame underscores a vital lesson: when we refuse to take responsibility for our actions, we risk deepening our alienation from God and damaging the relationships we are entrusted to nurture and protect.

This infamous question, "Am I my brother's keeper?" serves as a timeless warning, drawing attention to our responsibility toward others—especially those closest to us. As members of the human family, we are indeed our "brother's keeper," entrusted with the care and well-being of those around us and accountable for how we treat them. Cain's refusal to acknowledge this obligation starkly contrasts with the biblical principle of love and care for others. His actions highlight the devastating consequences of choosing jealousy, dishonesty, and evasion over humility, responsibility, and repentance. As a result, his life was forever marked by the weight of his choices, leading to a life of exile and alienation.

Cain's story serves as a powerful warning, illustrating how unchecked jealousy can escalate into unimaginable evil. It underscores the dangers of allowing jealousy to fester and highlights the importance of taking responsibility for our actions, especially in our relationships with others. By refusing to be his brother's keeper, Cain forfeited his relationship with Abel and damaged his relationship with Jehovah, leaving his life marked by the painful consequences of sin.

Jealousy Sold A Boy Into Slavery

Joseph's success similarly sparked jealousy, and like Abel, this was also among his own brothers. Favored by his father and blessed with prophetic dreams, Joseph's position as the chosen one in the family created deep resentment.

In Genesis 37:7, we see young Joseph eagerly sharing his divinely inspired dream with his brothers. It's easy to imagine the scene—Joseph, full of childlike innocence and naivety, approaching his siblings with excitement, completely believing they would share in his joy. This image is one we can all relate to. As children, we often couldn't wait to share something wonderful—a new discovery, an exciting experience, or a small triumph—with our friends or family. Their responses were equally innocent and enthusiastic, as they celebrated alongside us without hesitation.

Yet, as we grow older, this dynamic often changes. The pure, unfiltered joy we once experienced in sharing good news begins to fade. Instead of the unreserved delight we might expect, we may encounter indifference or, worse, resentment. What happened to the spontaneous excitement and shared happiness of our younger years? Why do relationships become increasingly complicated as we grow older?

Societal influences and cultural norms often shape how relationships evolve over time. The increasing emphasis on individual achievement and societal pressures to "keep up" can foster competition, making it harder to celebrate others' successes. Cultural expectations, such as prioritizing personal ambition or material success, can erode the mutual support and simplicity that once defined childhood relationships. These factors often compel individuals to measure their worth through comparisons, further complicating adult dynamics.

Relationships, once rooted in simplicity, become entangled with comparison, competition, and insecurities. While children naturally seek connection and mutual joy, adults often carry the weight of societal pressures, personal struggles, and unspoken rivalries. Unfortunately, this can overshadow our ability to genuinely rejoice in others' successes, leaving envy or self-doubt in its place.

Joseph's brothers illustrate this transformation. Admittedly, the tension in their relationship was already present; Genesis 37:2 notes that Joseph had brought a bad report about them to their father. Such history likely compounded their feelings. However, all things being equal, rather than delighting in their younger brother's dreams, they allowed jealousy to consume them. Instead of seeing his vision as a hopeful promise, they viewed it as a threat to their own standing. This inability to celebrate Joseph's joy shows that, as relationships mature, preserving the innocence and mutual support of childhood requires deliberate effort.

This reflection reminds us to resist letting life's complexities erode our capacity to celebrate the success and blessings of others. By striving to preserve a childlike purity in our relationships—one that is free from envy and full of love—we can build connections that inspire and uplift. As Jesus said in Matthew 18:3,

> "Truly I say to you, unless you turn around and become as young children, you will by no means enter into the Kingdom of the heavens." —Matthew 18:3

Cultivating such childlike hearts allows us to find joy in the happiness of others and fosters relationships that reflect the love Jehovah desires us to show.

The brothers, consumed by jealousy over Joseph's favored position and his prophetic dreams, plotted against him. Their jealousy, like Cain's, did not remain a quiet feeling of discontent —it grew into a murderous intent. Initially, Joseph's brothers wanted to kill him outright, as Genesis 37:18 reveals. They saw Joseph, a boy of 17 years old, approaching from a distance and conspired to take his life. The mere sight of him, a reminder of their father's favoritism and God's blessing, ignited such hatred in their hearts that even the bond of brotherhood did not restrain their wicked intentions.

Here too, as seen in the first murder ever committed, family ties, which should have been a source of love and protection, were not enough to hold back the destructive power of jealousy. Even though they ultimately chose to sell Joseph into slavery rather than kill him, this decision did not stem from any renewed sense of family loyalty. It was purely pragmatic—they wanted to rid themselves of Joseph without staining their hands with his blood. The fact that these brothers were willing to contemplate murder again shows how jealousy can erode even the strongest natural bonds, turning family members into mortal enemies.

Jealousy drove them to separate their brother from the family and caused heartache to their father. Though Joseph survived and eventually rose to prominence, the pain of his brothers' betrayal was a wound that surely could not be easily healed. Their actions demonstrate the dangerous lengths to which jealousy can drive people, illustrating how envy clouds judgment and compels individuals, even siblings, to take actions they might never have considered under normal circumstances.

Jealousy Devoured A King

David's success in battle and the favor he earned from the people stirred jealousy—not from family members in his case, but from a king. This shift in the individual harboring jealousy reveals how jealousy respects no boundaries of stature or position. Even someone as powerful and established as King Saul, the leader of Israel, was not immune to the destructive power of jealousy. Despite David's loyalty and faithfulness, Saul viewed David's rising popularity and military victories as a direct threat to his own reign. Saul's jealousy quickly took root and grew into an obsession that harmed his relationship with David and ultimately led to his own demise.

This account of Saul reveals that jealousy is a universal emotion, deeply ingrained in human nature. No matter how high a person rises or how secure their position might seem, envy can still creep in and take control. Saul had everything one might desire—power, wealth, respect—yet even he could not escape the grip of jealousy. David's success on the battlefield, his favor with the people, and his reputation as a man blessed by Jehovah stirred insecurity in Saul.

Saul's early humility is evident in the account of his anointing as king. When he was first chosen, he viewed himself as unworthy of such a high position, even hiding among the baggage when presented to the people (1 Samuel 10:22). This humility marked the beginning of his reign and endeared him to the nation. However, as time passed, jealousy and pride eroded these qualities. This tragic shift between Saul's initial humility and his later downfall starkly demonstrates how unrestrained jealousy can dismantle the very virtues that once defined a person's character.

Instead of focusing on his own responsibilities as king and maintaining a strong relationship with God, Saul fixated on David's growing popularity. His jealousy transformed him into a paranoid and violent ruler, consumed with the fear of losing his power and position. It drove him to attempt to kill David multiple times and ultimately led to his downfall, as he prioritized his envy over his relationship with God (1 Samuel 18:7-11; 19:1). The king's fear of being overshadowed by David revealed a weakness that even his royal position could not protect him from: the vulnerability of human pride and ego.

Jealousy, as seen in Saul's case, often blinds individuals to the good qualities and intentions of others. Despite David's unwavering loyalty to Saul, the king saw David as an enemy. David had repeatedly shown his faithfulness, refusing to harm Saul even when given the opportunity to do so (1 Samuel 24:10), but Saul's jealousy distorted his perception of David's actions. This highlights a significant aspect of jealousy—it can erode rational thought and judgment. Instead of appreciating David's loyalty and the way David was strengthening Israel's defenses through his military successes, Saul viewed him through a lens of suspicion and paranoia. His obsession with eliminating David became all-consuming, blurring the lines between friend and foe.

As demonstrated in the account of Saul, jealousy has the power to corrupt even the most established and revered individuals. God chose Saul to be the first king of Israel, a role of immense honor and responsibility. Yet, despite his initial humility and the divine support he received early in his reign, Saul allowed jealousy to overshadow his achievements and tarnish his legacy. His fixation on David prevented him from focusing on his role as king and led him to make reckless decisions that destabilized his kingdom.

Instead of acting as a strong, wise leader, Saul became erratic, obsessed with removing David as a perceived threat. His jealousy was so overwhelming that it caused him to neglect his duties, bringing turmoil to Israel and setting the stage for further conflict. Saul's kingship should have been a source of confidence and strength, but his inability to control his jealousy eroded his judgment and stability. It shows that even those with great power can be undone by envy if they allow it to fester. Saul's tragic end—marked by desperation, fear, and eventual rejection by Jehovah—serves as a sobering reminder that unrestrained jealousy can destroy relationships, as well as personal and professional stability.

In addition to destabilizing Saul's reign, his jealousy also brought widespread turmoil to the nation of Israel. The kingdom, which should have been united under a strong and focused leader, became fractured by Saul's personal vendetta against David. His jealousy led him to divert time and resources from governing the nation to pursuing David, creating unrest and uncertainty within the kingdom. This broader impact of Saul's jealousy underscores how envy can spread its destructive influence beyond personal relationships, affecting entire communities, organizations, or nations. When leaders or individuals in positions of authority are consumed by envy, it weakens their effectiveness and undermines the stability of those in their care.

Saul's tragic story serves as a timeless warning of how envy can blind individuals to the good in others, compromising their judgment, and ultimately leading to their downfall. It highlights the importance of embracing humility and celebrating the successes of others rather than envying them. Practical steps for cultivating and maintaining humility to prevent outcomes such as Saul's are explored further in Chapter 5. His jealousy prevented him from recognizing and valuing David's loyalty and faithfulness—qualities that should have been embraced, not feared. By allowing envy to take root, Saul forfeited the stability of his reign and undermined the very relationships that could have strengthened his leadership.

Ultimately, the story of King Saul vividly illustrates the pervasive and far-reaching nature of jealousy—it spares no one. Jealousy is not confined to personal relationships; its effects ripple outward, spreading discord and instability to those around. It transcends social status, power, and wealth, affecting both kings and common people alike. Saul's downfall serves as a warning that, regardless of one's success or rank, unchecked jealousy can cloud judgment, harm relationships, and tarnish even the most enduring legacies.

Chapter 4: The Success Paradox

S uccess is often celebrated as the pinnacle of achievement, bringing rewards, recognition, and respect. Yet,

> *"The worst part of success is trying to find someone who is happy for you." —Bette Midler*

As Bette Midler points out in the quote above and as discussed in Chapter 3, success can trigger feelings of envy in others. Success often brings with it the challenge of finding genuine support from those around us. The journey to success can be exhilarating, but reaching it may reveal complex social dynamics that make the experience bittersweet.

While one's achievements might initially be met with praise, success can also evoke feelings of resentment. This often-hidden reality—where admiration can turn to envy and relationships can sour—is what makes success unexpectedly isolating for many. People who once cheered for your progress may feel threatened or overshadowed by your accomplish-ments, making it difficult to find those who are truly happy for you.

The Dual Nature Of Success

Like a silent venom, jealousy can creep into hearts and minds, often disguised as frustration, comparison, or insecurity. The greater the success, the louder jealousy's intoxicating call can become, and the more difficult it can be to resist its destructive influence. This is the unfortunate paradox of success: it has the power to inspire both admiration and envy simultaneously. The very qualities that attract respect can also provoke jealousy. This duality reveals the complex social and emotional dynamics surrounding success. The very qualities that make success appealing can also turn it into a breeding ground for jealousy's corrosive grip. In an ironic twist, success —typically seen as a positive force—can at the same time become a source of negativity for both the successful person and those around them.

Jealousy's call becomes intoxicating because it taps into deeply rooted human emotions—pride, insecurity, and the need for validation. It clouds the ability to see the hard work, integrity, or faithfulness that often leads to genuine success, and instead, it fuels feelings of competition and rivalry. It whispers the lie that another person's success diminishes our own worth, creating a false narrative of scarcity. When someone sees another person's achievements, they may feel as though there is less opportunity for them to succeed, as if success were a limited resource. This mindset fuels jealousy, turning what could be admiration or inspiration into alienation and condemnation.

As discussed in Chapter 3, the success of Abel, Joseph, and David spurred jealousy that went beyond mere resentment. It became a driving force that led to acts of betrayal, cruelty, and even murder. Instead of focusing on their own growth or seeking to improve their relationship with God, Cain, Joseph's brothers, and Saul allowed jealousy to dominate their hearts and minds. Jealousy skewed their perception, making them see those blessed by Jehovah as rivals rather than examples of faithfulness to emulate.

These accounts serve as sobering reminders of the potential dangers of success. When success provokes jealousy in others, it can distort judgment, poison relationships, and lead to grievous actions. Instead of celebrating the success of others or using it as an opportunity for self-reflection and strengthening their relationship with God, those consumed by jealousy often choose destructive paths. This underscores the importance of guarding our hearts against envy, and remembering that God's blessings are not a finite resource. Each person's success should remind us of God's generosity and serve as a source of encouragement, not rivalry.

The intoxicating call of jealousy can poison entire communities, workplaces, or even congregations when one person's success is met with envy instead of support. Jealousy stirs up division, creates unnecessary competition, and undermines unity. It can make even the most capable individuals feel threatened, insecure, or inadequate, leading to actions that harm others and diminish their own integrity.

I know of a case where a team member was passed over for a promotion, and an external candidate was appointed instead. This decision sparked jealousy among the team, leading to resentment and efforts to undermine the new manager's authority. The environment became so toxic that several employees resigned, and more than half the team was eventually let go. This real-world scenario mirrors lessons from biblical accounts, demonstrating how envy can corrode unity and trust.

The call of jealousy is strong because it taps into the human desire for validation and worth. However, by guarding our hearts and focusing on spiritual pursuits and our relationship with God, we can resist this destructive influence. Instead of being seduced by jealousy, we can draw inspiration from the success of others, using it as a reminder of what is possible when we remain faithful, diligent, and aligned with God's principles. Chapter 1 highlights the value of true success and how it fosters a spirit of encouragement, unity, and gratitude in everything we do.

The remedy for jealousy's seductive call is found in shifting our focus away from comparison and toward appreciation. By celebrating the success of others and recognizing it as a result of their hard work, faithfulness, or blessings from God, we disarm jealousy's power. Success does not have to be a zero-sum game. When we view life from a spiritual perspective, understanding that God's blessings are abundant and not limited, we can replace envy with gratitude and encouragement.

Ultimately, Abel, Joseph, and David remind us in Chapter 1 that while faithfulness to God leads to true success, it may also attract opposition from others. However, even in the face of such challenges, they remained committed to their relationship with God, trusting Him to handle the difficulties they encountered. Their examples encourage us to focus on what truly matters: our faithfulness to Jehovah, regardless of how others may react to our success.

Do Not Shrink Back

Since success has a paradoxical nature—inviting admiration and inspiring motivation, yet often sparking jealousy—how can we avoid causing others to stumble? Should we limit ourselves out of fear of inciting jealousy? Absolutely not! Each of us has a responsibility—an obligation—to pursue success by giving our best in every endeavor.

Holding back our efforts to excel out of concern for provoking envy in others would be a disservice to the abilities, resources, and opportunities entrusted to us. Striving for success honors these gifts, demonstrating gratitude and stewardship. Whether in personal growth, secular work, or spiritual pursuits, failing to give our best would mean neglecting our responsibilities and falling short of the potential that God has given us.

> "We are all meant to shine, as children do. It's not just in some of us; it's in everyone. And as we let our own light shine, we unconsciously give other people permission to do the same." —Marianne Williamson

Williamson reminds us that holding back from our true potential doesn't protect or help others; it limits both us and those around us. By embracing our strengths and striving for success, we create an atmosphere in which others feel inspired and empowered to pursue their own growth. Our achievements and efforts to excel don't have to be sources of division or envy; rather, they can serve as beacons of possibility. When we shine, we demonstrate what is possible, encouraging others to rise to their own unique callings rather than shrinking in fear or comparison.

Doing our best is about more than personal achievement; it's about honoring God by imitating His qualities of diligence, integrity, and excellence. Ecclesiastes 9:10 emphasizes that:

> "Whatever your hand finds to do, do with all your might." — Ecclesiastes 9:10

This counsel urges us to pour our full energy and enthusiasm into every assignment. Rather than measuring our efforts by human praise or worrying about others' reactions, we are to devote ourselves wholeheartedly so that our actions reflect Jehovah's excellence and bring genuine, lasting honor to Him.

The Courage To Shine

The Bible encourages us not to let fear of others' reactions hold us back. In fact, Hebrews 10:39 specifically calls us to "not shrink back." The apostle Paul originally applied this principle to boldness in sharing the good news of salvation through Christ. However, this courage also extends to other areas of life, provided our actions are not contrary to God's will. Whether it is standing firm for biblical principles, giving our best in every endeavor, or persevering through challenges, we are encouraged to move forward with confidence.

To "shrink back" would mean allowing fear of others or their reactions to dictate our actions, potentially leading to compromise or inaction. Such hesitation could show a lack of appreciation for the gifts and responsibilities God has entrusted to us, including our faith and the opportunity to serve Him.

By embracing this boldness, we demonstrate trust in God's support, as Paul reminds us: "*Jehovah is my helper; I will not be afraid. What can man do to me?*" (Hebrews 13:6). This confidence allows us to face challenges with courage and reflects our deep gratitude for His blessings. By refusing to shrink back, we can confidently pursue excellence, knowing that our efforts honor God and deepen our sense of purpose.

Proverbs 28:1 reminds us, "*But the righteous are as confident as a lion.*" This verse underscores that God expects us to move forward with courage, even in the face of potential opposition, criticism, or jealousy. Boldness, in this sense, is not recklessness but a courageous commitment to doing what is right, regardless of others' opinions or responses. It involves trusting that God will strengthen us and support our efforts as we seek to do His will.

This boldness is essential because it enables us to fully embrace our responsibilities and make the most of our opportunities. Rather than holding back due to fear of provoking jealousy, we are called to apply our gifts openly and without fear, knowing that God honors those who put their faith in Him. By being bold, we resist the temptation to hide our talents or minimize our efforts out of apprehension, and we avoid letting insecurity or external pressures undermine our resolve.

In the end, boldness in pursuing success aligns with our duty to reflect God's qualities of courage, resilience, and integrity. When we are bold, we show that we trust in God's guidance and believe in the purpose He has set for us. This courageous approach enables us to rise above any potential negativity, keeping our focus on fulfilling all our responsibilities—whether assigned externally or self-imposed from within—and honoring God through our actions.

We are also reminded that success achieved through diligence and integrity often brings benefits to those around us, not just to ourselves. When we excel, we may inspire others, contribute positively to our communities, and even encourage those who look to us for guidance. By striving to do our best, we set an example of hard work and faithfulness, qualities that can uplift and motivate others who witness our efforts.

While some may react to our success with envy, we should not let this discourage us from fully pursuing our goals. Instead, we are encouraged not to pursue success at the expense of alienating others. We will explore the importance of remaining humble and focusing on our intentions in Chapter 5, ensuring that our aim is not to overshadow others but to faithfully fulfill the roles and responsibilities that God has assigned to us.

By doing so, we avoid falling into pride and stay focused on the larger purpose behind our efforts. This commitment to doing our best transforms success into something far greater than personal gain—it becomes an act of integrity and faithfulness. In this way, our efforts gain lasting value and contribute meaningfully to the greater good, even in the face of challenges.

Balancing Rewards And Challenges

Success is a multi-faceted journey that demands both resilience and discernment. While it presents challenges, including the risk of provoking envy, it also provides opportunities to exhibit Jehovah's qualities of diligence, humility, and love, reminding us of the greater purpose behind our efforts. By maintaining a spirit of gratitude and staying focused on our spiritual goals, we can rise above the complexities of success and inspire others to do the same. Rather than viewing success as a zero-sum game, we can embrace it as an avenue to glorify God and promote harmony within our communities.

Ultimately, we must acknowledge the emotional complexity that success can bring. Recognizing this reality allows us to approach success with both humility and resilience, remaining mindful of the impact our achievements may have on our relationships and being prepared to navigate both the rewards and challenges it entails. Let us, then, resolve to never "shrink back," trusting that Jehovah will bless our efforts when we remain steadfast in doing His will.

Understanding the paradox of success helps us navigate its challenges. In the next chapter, we will explore practical ways to foster unity and prevent envy from arising.

Chapter 5: How To Avoid Provoking Jealousy

N avigating success and personal blessings often requires a balanced approach, especially when we consider how our actions may affect those around us. While it is neither honorable nor righteous to limit our goals, growth, or contributions out of fear of provoking jealousy, it is wise to be mindful of the impact our success may have on others. Recognizing jealousy's potential to harm relationships helps us approach our own accomplishments with thoughtfulness, encouraging a mindset that promotes unity rather than rivalry.

This chapter focuses primarily on external relationships—how our actions and expressions of success can either defuse or intensify feelings of jealousy in others. Taking practical steps to avoid provoking jealousy is not about suppressing our joy or achievements, but rather about creating an environment where others feel valued and respected. By cultivating humility, practicing generosity, and being mindful in our interactions, we can foster unity and strengthen bonds.

For internal strategies to manage jealousy within ourselves, such as overcoming feelings of inadequacy or comparison, see Chapter 6. Together, these two chapters offer a comprehensive approach to understanding and addressing jealousy from both external and internal perspectives.

1. Share Generously

> *"We make a living by what we get, but we make a life by what we give."* —Winston Churchill

An effective approach to avoiding the provocation of jealousy is to share our blessings generously. As Churchill aptly stated, our lives gain true meaning through giving. When we extend our resources, time, and kindness to others, we create inclusion and unity that help diminish feelings of envy. The early Christians exemplified this spirit of generosity by sharing everything they had, so that "*no one was in need among them*" (Acts 4:32-35). Their willingness to share their possessions fostered a powerful sense of community, allowing each member to feel supported and valued, regardless of personal wealth or status.

In the biblical book of Genesis, Abraham demonstrated this same spirit of generosity in his dealings with his nephew Lot. As their families and possessions grew, tensions arose between their herdsmen over limited grazing land. Abraham took the initiative to resolve the conflict peacefully. Despite being the elder and having the right to choose first, Abraham humbly said to Lot, "*Please, let there be no quarreling between me and you and between my herders and your herders, for we are brothers. Is not the whole land available to you? Please separate from me. If you go to the left, I will go to the right; but if you go to the right, I will go to the left.*" (Genesis 13:8-9).

Abraham's generosity defused a potential family conflict and reinforced the bond between him and Lot. By prioritizing peace over personal gain, Abraham showed Lot that he valued their relationship more than material possessions. Although the Bible emphasizes Abraham's generosity and goodwill more prominently, Lot's peaceful response to Abraham's leadership and his acceptance of the arrangement indicate a level of respect and loyalty that also contributed to their relationship. Lot's willingness to work harmoniously with Abraham reflected his appreciation for Abraham's integrity and further solidified their family bond.

Another example of the power of generosity, though with a different outcome, is found in the account of Jacob and Laban. When Jacob requested to leave Laban's household to support his own family, they struck an agreement regarding the flocks. Jacob would take only the speckled, spotted, and dark-colored animals as his wages while Laban kept the rest.

Through divine blessing and Jacob's strategic breeding, the flocks that were his share grew abundantly. This increase, though rightful, provoked jealousy in Laban and his sons, as noted in Genesis 31:1-2, where they accused Jacob of taking their father's wealth. In this case, Jacob's hard work and blessings did not prevent jealousy from taking root. However, Jacob maintained his integrity and left the outcome in God's hands. Jehovah blessed Jacob with abundant possessions and protected him, ultimately instructing him to leave Laban's household and guiding him to safety (Genesis 31:3, 24).

This shows that while sharing and generosity can often diffuse tension and prevent jealousy, as it did in the case of Abraham and Lot, it may not always yield the same result, as seen with Jacob and Laban. Nevertheless, acting with integrity and sharing generously brings rewards, as God sees and blesses those who act in harmony with His principles.

Moreover, a spirit of generosity reflects gratitude for what we have received and acknowledges that our blessings are gifts rather than entitlements. By sharing these gifts with others, we strengthen our relationships and foster an environment where everyone feels a part of each other's successes. As 1 Timothy 6:18 encourages,

> *"Tell them to work at good, to be rich in fine works, to be generous, ready to share." —1 Timothy 6:18*

Abraham's selfless generosity and Jacob's trust in God, along with their desire to maintain harmony, brought peace and blessings to their lives and set an example of humility and faith.

These accounts remind us that while generosity may not always prevent jealousy, it reflects a spirit of love and righteousness that pleases God. By focusing on collective well-being, we can build relationships rooted in trust and mutual respect, knowing that Jehovah rewards those who act in harmony with His will.

2. Humility

> *"True humility is not thinking less of yourself; it is thinking of yourself less." —C.S. Lewis*

To avoid provoking jealousy, one essential quality is maintaining humility. Humility keeps us grounded, preventing us from seeking admiration or flaunting our achievements in ways that might stir envy in others. Jesus exemplified this humility perfectly. Despite having unparalleled authority, he *"did not even consider the idea of trying to be equal to God,"* but rather *"emptied himself and took a slave's form,"* living among humans with gentleness and modesty (Philippians 2:6-8). Jesus' humility made him approachable and relatable, drawing people to him without provoking resentment or jealousy.

In Chapter 3, Saul's inability to remain humble, despite starting off modestly, illustrates how jealousy can destroy a person. On the other hand, Jonathan, King Saul's son, serves as a great example of humility. Even though he was the heir to the throne, he acknowledged that God had chosen David to be king. Jonathan demonstrated selflessness by making a loyalty pact with David, which included giving David his royal robe, armor, sword, bow, and belt—symbols of his status as the crown prince (1 Samuel 18:3-4). This act was not merely symbolic; it reflected Jonathan's recognition of God's plan and his support for David. Their friendship grew stronger as a result of this humility, fostering trust and mutual respect.

Their bond was so profound that when they had to separate for their safety, it affected them deeply. They cried together during their farewell, with David weeping the hardest (1 Samuel 20:41-42). This moment reveals how significant their friendship was, thanks to Jonathan's humility and his willingness to prioritize David's safety over his own.

Jonathan's humility had lasting effects and endeared him to David, forging a connection that transcended personal ambitions. After Jonathan's death, David honored their friendship by being kind to Jonathan's son, Mephibosheth. He restored Mephibosheth's family inheritance and ensured that he always had a place at the king's table (2 Samuel 9:1-7). David's kindness reflected Jonathan's humility and created a legacy of loyalty and goodwill for future generations.

Jonathan's story teaches us that humility builds relationships based on trust, loyalty, and care. By placing God's will ahead of his own desires, Jonathan fostered a friendship that brought strength to both him and David, leaving a lasting heritage of love and unity.

Humility naturally leads us to focus on others rather than drawing attention to ourselves. When we downplay our successes and highlight the contributions of others, we foster an environment where people feel appreciated and valued rather than diminished by comparison. Proverbs 27:2 reminds us,

> "Let someone else praise you, and not your own mouth." — Proverbs 27:2

By choosing modesty, we deflect attention and avoid inadvertently sparking feelings of jealousy in those around us. This approach encourages unity, as it shows respect for others' abilities and acknowledges that all success ultimately comes from God.

Furthermore, true humility reminds us that our talents and blessings are not solely our own accomplishments but gifts from Jehovah. Recognizing this can help us avoid boastfulness and instead express gratitude, attributing our achievements to divine support rather than personal ability. This attitude of gratitude and humility, exemplified by Jesus and Jonathan and emphasized throughout Scripture, protects our relationships, promotes peace, and helps prevent jealousy from taking root in our interactions with others.

3. Acknowledge Others' Contributions

> "Appreciation is a wonderful thing: It makes what is excellent in others belong to us as well." —Voltaire

When we openly recognize the efforts and talents of those around us, we foster an appreciation and respect that helps reduce feelings of envy. The apostle Paul set an excellent example of this in his letters, often going out of his way to commend his fellow workers by name and express gratitude for their specific efforts (Romans 16:1-16). By highlighting their unique roles and contributions, Paul demonstrated that he valued each person's efforts as essential to the overall health of the congregation.

Recognizing others' contributions allows people to feel seen and appreciated, reinforcing the notion that their efforts matter. This acknowledgment helps shift the focus away from individual achievements and toward collective success, creating an atmosphere where everyone feels they have an important role to play. By giving credit where it is due, we eliminate unnecessary comparisons, which can often be the root of jealousy. Instead of feeling overshadowed, others can take pride in the fact that their work is valued and celebrated, thereby reducing the likelihood of resentment.

This principle is beautifully illustrated in the account of Moses and Joshua. As Moses approached the end of his leadership of Israel, God directed him to appoint Joshua as his successor. Far from being territorial or possessive about his role, Moses humbly obeyed Jehovah's instructions and openly supported Joshua. Numbers 27:18-23 describes how Moses publicly laid his hands on Joshua in front of the entire congregation, recognizing God's choice and formally passing on the mantle of leadership.

This public acknowledgment of Joshua's role had a profound impact on both the nation of Israel and on Joshua himself. By openly endorsing him, Moses instilled confidence in Joshua as he stepped into his new position. Knowing that he had Moses' full support and the approval of God likely encouraged Joshua to lead with courage and humility. Later, as he led Israel into the Promised Land, God reassured him, saying, "Be courageous and strong. Do not be afraid or be terrified, for Jehovah your God is with you wherever you go." (Joshua 1:9)

Moses' acknowledgment of Joshua's role also reinforced trust and respect for Joshua among the Israelites, unifying them under his leadership. By ensuring that the nation witnessed this transfer of authority, Moses helped prevent potential challenges to Joshua's leadership, thereby fostering an atmosphere of cooperation and respect.

Furthermore, acknowledging contributions promotes humility in our own hearts. When we make it a habit to lift others up, we remind ourselves that success is rarely achieved alone. We begin to see accomplishments as the product of a supportive community rather than purely personal effort. As Philippians 2:3 encourages,

> "Do nothing out of contentiousness or out of egotism, but with humility consider others superior to you." — Philippians 2:3

This attitude fosters a collaborative spirit, demonstrating that we respect and cherish the unique gifts each individual brings. By recognizing others' efforts, as Moses did with Joshua, we cultivate an environment where everyone feels valued and included. This prevents jealousy and strengthens unity and mutual respect, thereby building relationships rooted in trust and appreciation. Moses' public recognition of Joshua's leadership undoubtedly played a significant role in Joshua's success, ensuring a smooth transition and creating a legacy of humility and effective leadership.

4. Respect In Sharing

> "A meaningful life is measured not by what we achieve, but by how much we encourage others to achieve." —Unknown

When we experience personal achievements or blessings, it's natural to want to share them with others. However, being mindful of how and when we share can help avoid stirring up feelings of jealousy. Proverbs 21:23 advises, "Whoever guards his mouth and his tongue keeps himself out of trouble." By being considerate in how we share our successes, we show respect and empathy toward others' circumstances. Before sharing news of a success, ask: Will this inspire or discourage those around me? This thoughtful approach doesn't mean hiding our accomplishments; rather, it means sharing them in ways that uplift rather than cause resentment.

A valuable example of the consequences of unmindful sharing is seen in the life of Hezekiah, the king of Judah. After recovering from a serious illness, Hezekiah received envoys from Babylon, sent by King Merodach-baladan. Flattered by their visit, Hezekiah displayed all his treasures, including silver, gold, spices, and weapons, saying, *"There is nothing that I did not show them in my storehouses."* (Isaiah 39:4). However, his lack of discretion had serious consequences. The prophet Isaiah foretold that one day Babylon would carry off all the treasures Hezekiah had so proudly displayed, along with some of his descendants. This prophecy was fulfilled during the Babylonian exile (2 Kings 20:12-19).

Hezekiah's story serves as a reminder of the importance of discernment in sharing our blessings. While his intentions may not have been malicious, his actions exposed Judah's wealth and strength to a future enemy. This underscores the need for thoughtfulness about how we share our blessings, especially with those who might misuse the information for their advantage.

Similarly, the account of Joseph illustrates how unguarded sharing can provoke jealousy. When Joseph shared his dreams of future greatness with his brothers, who already felt overshadowed, their jealousy intensified (Genesis 37:5-11). Though Joseph's dreams were true and meaningful, his lack of sensitivity in sharing them caused strife within his family. Both Hezekiah and Joseph remind us that, while sharing blessings can be joyful, we must always consider how our words may affect others, especially if they feel vulnerable or overlooked.

Being mindful also means discerning the timing and context of sharing good news. Ecclesiastes 3:7 reminds us that there is "a time to speak" and a time to be silent. For instance, if someone close to us is struggling with a setback, it may be better to hold back on sharing news about our own success until they are in a better place emotionally. This doesn't diminish our joy but shows compassion and patience, reinforcing the strength of our relationships.

Another important aspect of mindful sharing is using our blessings to encourage others. For example, instead of solely highlighting our accomplishments, we could share the challenges we faced along the way, emphasizing that our success wasn't immediate or without difficulties. This can make our experiences more relatable and encouraging, especially for those who might be feeling discouraged. Philippians 2:4 encourages us to be mindful of others' well-being with the advice to

> *"Look out not only for your own interests, but also for the interests of others."* —Philippians 2:4

Ultimately, when we approach sharing with humility and empathy, we avoid coming across as boastful or insensitive. This allows us to rejoice in our blessings without jeopardizing relationships. As Romans 12:15 encourages, *"Rejoice with those who rejoice; weep with those who weep."* By following this counsel, we build bonds that are grounded in mutual respect and understanding, making it easier for others to rejoice with us in our times of success.

5. Encourage Teamwork

> *"Coming together is a beginning, staying together is progress, and working together is success."* —Henry Ford

Encouraging a spirit of collaboration rather than rivalry can go a long way in reducing jealousy. When we emphasize collaboration, we highlight that each person's contribution is valuable and essential to the group's success. This approach aligns with Ecclesiastes 4:9, which states, *"Two are better than one because they have a good reward for their hard work."* By fostering collaboration, we show that success is often achieved best when we work together, rather than by competing against each other.

Jesus' teachings to his disciples often emphasized unity over competition. In Luke 9:46-48, when the disciples argued about who among them was the greatest, Jesus gently corrected them, teaching that true greatness comes from humility and service. He redirected their focus from competing with one another to supporting each other in fulfilling Jehovah's purpose. Jesus' counsel demonstrates that encouraging collaboration rather than comparison helps us focus on shared goals, making jealousy less likely to arise.

In practical terms, encouraging collaboration means looking for ways to involve others in our projects and achievements. For instance, when we work on something exciting, inviting others to contribute their skills or perspectives strengthens the outcome and allows them to share in the joy of success. Romans 12:10 says, *"In brotherly love have tender affection for one another. In showing honor to one another, take the lead."* When we honor others' abilities and contributions, it builds a cooperative environment where everyone feels valued.

This principle is exemplified in the construction of the tabernacle during Israel's journey through the wilderness. God specifically chose Bezalel and Oholiab, along with other skilled craftsmen, to oversee the work (Exodus 35:30-35). Each worker contributed their unique skills—whether in weaving, metalworking, or woodworking—to create a structure that was beautiful and worthy of God's presence. This collaboration ensured the project's success and emphasized the importance of each individual's contribution. By fostering a spirit of teamwork, jealousy was avoided, as each craftsman recognized that their role was integral to the greater purpose. This aligns with the principle in 1 Peter 4:10, which acknowledges that each person's talents are gifts to be used for the benefit of others, as it states,

> *"To the extent that each one has received a gift, use it in ministering to one another as fine stewards of God's undeserved kindness that is expressed in various ways." —1 Peter 4:10*

Another biblical example of collaboration over competition is seen in the early Christian congregation. Acts 2:44-45 shows that the early Christians *"were together and had all things in common."* They pooled their resources and worked together to support each other, which fostered a spirit of unity and discouraged jealousy. By sharing what they had and contributing to one another's well-being, they were able to build a community based on love and support rather than rivalry.

When we prioritize collaboration, we create a culture that values each person's role. This makes it easier for everyone to celebrate one another's achievements without envy, as they recognize that everyone's success contributes to the greater good. This approach helps us achieve more collectively, strengthens bonds, and reduces feelings of jealousy, reinforcing the unity and love that Jesus desired among his followers (John 13:34-35).

A Path To Unity And Peace

Cultivating an environment where jealousy is less likely to arise requires a thoughtful, deliberate approach rooted in love, humility, and generosity. The practical steps outlined—sharing generously, maintaining humility, acknowledging others' contributions, being respectful in sharing, and encouraging teamwork over competition—serve as valuable tools for building stronger, healthier relationships. These principles reflect the spirit of Christ's teachings, fostering unity and mutual respect while helping us avoid unnecessary tension and resentment. While this chapter addresses external dynamics, Chapter 6 delves deeper into overcoming internal feelings of jealousy.

Ultimately, navigating personal success and blessings with care isn't about downplaying our achievements; it's about honoring the relationships we value and maintaining peace with those around us. By being mindful of how we interact with others, we can cultivate a spirit of encouragement and support that uplifts everyone involved. This approach preserves the bonds of love and trust while reflecting our desire to emulate God's qualities and live according to His principles.

When we strive to live with humility and generosity, we foster harmony in our relationships and create a foundation of mutual joy. By doing so, we honor Jehovah, strengthen our relationships, and experience the profound peace that comes from walking in harmony with His Word. Ultimately, fostering unity over rivalry leads to richer, more meaningful connections and a deeper sense of fulfillment in our lives.

Chapter 6: How To Rid Yourself Of Jealousy

J ust as we aim to be considerate of others' feelings when we experience success, we also face the challenge of managing our own feelings when others succeed. Seeing friends, family, or colleagues achieve something we desire can stir up feelings of jealousy or inadequacy within us, even if we genuinely want the best for them. This emotional struggle is common and doesn't make us unkind; rather, it reflects our desire for growth and our yearning for similar accomplishments in our own lives.

Candidly recognizing these feelings is the first step toward a more supportive mindset. Just as we would want others to celebrate our achievements without resentment, we must also learn to celebrate theirs, seeing their success as an inspiration rather than a threat. In doing so, we cultivate an environment where encouragement and genuine happiness for others can become second nature.

Managing jealousy isn't about suppressing our own dreams or diminishing our desires; it's about cultivating a heart that finds joy in the successes of others while trusting in God's unique plan for our own rewards and accomplishments. This approach deepens our relationships and liberates us to focus on our own journeys. The apostle Paul emphasized the value of contentment when he wrote, "So, *having food and clothing, we will be content with these things*" (1 Timothy 6:8). When we embrace this mindset, we are reminded that true satisfaction doesn't come from comparison but from appreciating what God provides. By shifting our focus from competition to collaboration, we transform moments of envy into opportunities for growth, building stronger, more supportive bonds with those around us.

1. Pray And Personal Study

Prayer is one of the most important ways to seek God's guidance, especially when battling emotions like jealousy. Through heartfelt communication with God, we can share our deepest feelings, knowing that He cares and understands. When jealousy stirs within us, it can be easy to feel ashamed or conflicted, but God invites us to approach Him openly, regardless of our feelings. He is *"near to all those calling on Him"* (Psalm 145:18), ready to listen without judgment and to offer the support we need.

Philippians 4:6-7 encourages us, saying:

> *"Do not be anxious over anything, but in everything by prayer and supplication along with thanksgiving let your petitions be made known to God; and the peace of God that surpasses all understanding will guard your hearts and your mental powers by means of Christ Jesus."* — *Philippians 4:6-7*

This scripture highlights two key promises. First, Jehovah offers us His peace, a gift beyond all understanding. This peace doesn't depend on external circumstances; rather, it steadies our hearts from within, allowing us to see past jealousy's influence. Second, this peace acts as a guard, protecting our hearts and minds from being overwhelmed by negative emotions.

Through prayer, we can ask God to replace feelings of jealousy with more positive emotions. For instance, we might request help to feel joy over the successes of others or to focus on our own blessings. When we express these desires sincerely, God responds by helping to reshape our hearts, enabling us to feel peace, gratitude, and serenity. Instead of viewing a situation solely through the lens of what we lack or wish we had, He helps us see things through the perspective of contentment and appreciation.

As we continue to turn to Jehovah in prayer, we build trust in Him and deepen our relationship with Him. This practice gradually helps us rise above jealousy, transforming our hearts to reflect qualities such as love, kindness, and compassion. In this way, prayer is not just a source of comfort; it's an active tool that God offers us to reshape our inner selves, leading us toward the serenity and clarity that only He can provide.

> "Your word is a lamp to my foot, and a light for my path." — Psalm 119:105

Psalm 119:105 describes God's Word as a light that guides our way. This metaphor reminds us that the Bible illuminates our steps, helping us avoid stumbling into actions or attitudes that could harm ourselves or others. When jealousy clouds our perspective, studying the Bible offers insights and principles that guide us toward positive and spiritually healthy choices.

Proverbs 3:5 encourages us to "Trust in Jehovah with all your heart, and do not rely on your own understanding". This scripture reminds us of the limitations of human wisdom and the importance of relying on God for guidance, especially when dealing with complex emotions that can cloud our judgment. Seeking God's guidance through Bible study is, therefore, a powerful way to gain the wisdom needed to overcome negative emotions.

By studying the Bible, we also find good examples to imitate. Consider Jonathan, the son of King Saul. As David's popularity grew, Jonathan could have reasoned that David's success might jeopardize his own prospects for the throne. Yet, rather than feeling threatened and succumbing to jealousy, Jonathan formed a deep friendship with David (1 Samuel 18:1-4). His unselfish attitude highlights how love can overcome jealousy, offering us a positive example to follow. By reflecting on such accounts, we can gain practical strategies for managing jealousy with grace and maturity. We will explore Jonathan's account in greater detail in Chapter 12.

Moreover, Bible study connects us with God's thoughts and perspective. By understanding His loving nature, we are reminded of how He views each of us as unique and valuable. Studying the Bible can help us develop a balanced perspective, empowering us to find peace in our personal relationship with Jehovah.

Ultimately, Bible study is not just a source of knowledge but a means of transformation. When we reflect on the lessons, principles, and examples found in God's Word, our hearts and minds are gradually molded to reflect His qualities. This helps us to cultivate a spirit of love and kindness, building a positive environment for ourselves and those around us.

In essence, seeking God's guidance through prayer and Bible study helps us gain wisdom and draw closer to Him. This approach strengthens us to overcome jealousy and other negative feelings, cultivating a heart more aligned with God's qualities. In turn, this helps us foster a peaceful, positive environment both within ourselves and in our relationships with others.

2. Examine Your Motives

> *"What lies behind us and what lies before us are tiny matters compared to what lies within us." —Ralph Waldo Emerson*

Honestly examining our motives is a powerful way to address jealousy and cultivate a positive environment. Emerson's quote above aligns closely with the wisdom in 2 Corinthians 13:5, where the apostle Paul exhorts: *"Keep testing whether you are in the faith; keep proving what you yourselves are."* This scripture underscores the importance of regular self-examination to understand and refine our intentions.

When we examine our motives, we take a deeper look at the question *"why"* behind our feelings. Jealousy often stems from insecurities, comparisons, or unfulfilled desires. Without self-examination, these feelings can quietly influence our actions and attitudes, disrupting our peace and relationships. By asking ourselves questions like, *"Why am I feeling this way?"* or *"What am I hoping to achieve with these feelings?"* we can uncover hidden motivations, such as pride or dissatisfaction. This type of self-examination enables us to make adjustments, redirecting our hearts toward more positive and loving attitudes.

The importance of this reflective process is beautifully illustrated in Cain's account. God asked Cain why he was angry and dejected when he became downhearted in Genesis 4:6. This simple but powerful probing question encouraged Cain to pause and reflect on the root of his feelings. Was his anger truly justified, or was it driven by pride and jealousy?

Furthermore, examining our motives helps us align more closely with Jehovah's standards, fostering a heart of gratitude. Philippians 4:11 states, "*I have learned, in whatsoever state I am, therein to be content*" (ASV). By thoughtfully evaluating and adjusting our motives, we develop a heart that finds true satisfaction in God's provisions and timing, rather than yearning for what others possess.

Regular self-examination is like holding up a mirror to our hearts, much as described in the book of James. James 1:23-24 speaks of a man who looks at his face in a mirror, then walks away, immediately forgetting what he looks like. The scripture says,

> "*For if anyone is a hearer of the word and not a doer, this one is like a man looking at his own face in a mirror. For he looks at himself, and off he goes and immediately forgets what sort of person he is*". —James 1:23-24

This analogy highlights that simply glancing at our motives isn't enough; we need to remember what we observe and take meaningful action. Just as looking in a mirror helps us identify and address areas that need adjustment, examining our hearts can reveal where jealousy or envy may be lurking. A quick or superficial glance might cause us to miss critical insights and lose the opportunity to make necessary changes. Regular and thoughtful self-reflection helps us gain a clearer understanding of ourselves, which can motivate us to take deliberate steps toward improving our attitudes.

This self-reflection, combined with action, helps us foster an environment characterized by peace and kindness. In this way, we live out James' counsel—not merely hearing what the Bible says about purifying our motives but actively applying it. By holding ourselves to this standard, we cultivate a positive, harmonious atmosphere that reflects the love and unity God desires, rather than the discord and tension often caused by jealousy.

3. Appreciate Your Blessings

> "Do not spoil what you have by desiring what you have not; remember that what you now have was once among the things you only hoped for." —Epicurus

Regularly expressing gratitude shifts our perspective, helping us focus on what we have rather than dwelling on what we lack. This practice diminishes feelings of envy and fosters a positive, appreciative attitude. Psalm 103:1-5 beautifully encapsulates this principle, encouraging us to *"praise Jehovah"* and *"not forget all He has done,"* highlighting His acts of forgiveness, healing, and loving-kindness. When we take the time to reflect on the blessings we've received—whether spiritual, emotional, or material—we become less inclined to compare ourselves to others and more satisfied with God's provisions in our lives.

Gratitude reorients our focus and nurtures inner peace and satisfaction. Instead of allowing jealousy to creep in as we notice others' achievements or possessions, gratitude reminds us of the unique gifts we already possess. This shift in mindset helps us see our own value through the lens of God's generosity. By openly expressing thankfulness, we inspire those around us to do the same, creating an environment where happiness and joy naturally flourish. This ripple effect encourages a culture of gratitude, reducing jealousy and fostering mutual respect and appreciation.

For example, consider the account of Paul and Silas in prison (Acts 16:22-25). After being beaten and imprisoned, they could have easily felt resentment or envy toward those enjoying freedom. Instead, they prayed and sang songs of praise to God, demonstrating deep gratitude even in extreme adversity. Their positive attitude strengthened their faith and inspired those around them, including the jailer and his family, who ultimately became believers.

Similarly, the Israelites' experience with manna in the wilderness illustrates God's perfect provision. As recorded in Exodus 16:17-18, each household gathered just enough to meet their needs, regardless of family size or ability, and *"the one who had gathered much had no surplus, and the one who had gathered little had no shortage."*

Both accounts teach us that gratitude protects us from envy and resentment by helping us focus on God's sustaining care, even in the most challenging situations. Furthermore, when we cultivate gratitude, we create a positive foundation that strengthens relationships. Instead of focusing on achievements or possessions that could incite jealousy, we share our thankfulness with others, building a mutual appreciation and shared blessings.

Recognizing that our blessings are gifts from Jehovah fosters humility and gratitude, as we see them not as entitlements but as expressions of His kindness. This aligns with the counsel in James 1:17, which reminds us,

> *"Every good gift and every perfect present is from above, coming down from the Father of the celestial lights."* — James 1:17

Gratitude also transforms our outlook on challenges and unmet desires. Instead of fixating on what we lack, we can use gratitude as a tool to acknowledge the ways in which God sustains us through difficult times. This perspective helps us trust in His timing and wisdom, knowing that He provides exactly what we need when we need it. As we cultivate gratitude, we replace feelings of discontent with confidence in God's care, promoting lasting joy and spiritual stability.

Ultimately, gratitude enriches every aspect of our lives. It grounds us in fulfillment, strengthens our relationships, and helps us appreciate the diversity of God's gifts in our own lives and in the lives of others. By regularly practicing gratitude, we align our hearts with God's qualities, creating a life filled with peace, humility, and genuine happiness.

4. Concentrate On Your Responsibilities

Focusing on our assigned responsibilities is a powerful way to guard against harboring jealousy. The apostle Paul encourages us to:

> "Let us not become egotistical, stirring up competition with one another, envying one another." —Galatians 5:26.

The advice in Galatians 5:26 is especially relevant when we find ourselves tempted to compare our circumstances or achievements with those of others. By focusing on our own assignments, we can avoid the pitfalls of jealousy and experience greater peace and satisfaction.

When we concentrate on our unique roles, we are reminded of our individual value and purpose. Each person has his or her own set of abilities and experiences, and Jehovah, as a loving Father, provides each of us with opportunities that are best suited to our strengths. Recognizing this can help us appreciate our own path rather than feeling envious of someone else's. For example, if someone is entrusted with a particular role that we might desire, focusing on our own assignments can help us see the blessings in our current situations and prevent us from feeling less worthy or overlooked.

As 1 Corinthians 12:14-21 reminds us, we are all part of one body, each with a unique and essential function. We benefit by appreciating our unique "function," just as "the eye cannot say to the hand, 'I do not need you,'" nor can any part elevate itself above another. Each part has a purpose that contributes to the overall harmony of the body. Embracing this diversity of skills and experiences helps us realize that everyone—including ourselves—has a vital place in the bigger picture. When we view ourselves through this lens, we foster a deep sense of belonging and gratitude, knowing that our individual roles are meaningful and valued. This focus also helps us find joy in our assignments rather than in seeking approval or recognition from others.

A vivid example of this principle is seen in the rebuilding of Jerusalem's walls under Nehemiah's leadership. Nehemiah motivated each group to focus on its specific section, encouraging unity and cooperation. This collective effort led to the successful completion of what seemed like an impossible task: restoring the walls and gates of a ruined city despite constant threats from enemies. Remarkably, this monumental achievement was accomplished in just 52 days (Nehemiah 6:15). Their unity, hard work, and reliance on Jehovah demonstrated the extraordinary results that can be achieved when everyone faithfully fulfills their designated responsibilities.

> *"Don't aspire to be the best on the team. Aspire to be the best for the team." —Unkown*

Additionally, our goal should not be to outshine others but to faithfully carry out our assignments. When we focus on doing our best for the team, we can avoid feelings of inadequacy and resentment. Concentrating on our responsibilities reminds us that God values the quality of our efforts more than their visibility or scale. By focusing on what we have been given to do, we safeguard ourselves against feelings of inadequacy or resentment, appreciating the privilege of contributing in ways that align with our strengths.

This mindset also shifts our focus from recognition to genuine fulfillment. Jesus taught in Matthew 6:1-4 that acts of service performed in secret are highly valued by God. He assured his followers that God rewards not the public nature of our deeds but the sincerity and humility with which they are performed. This perspective helps us avoid seeking validation from others, allowing us to find satisfaction in knowing that our contributions please Jehovah.

Ultimately, centering our efforts on our own responsibilities allows us to experience true contentment. We avoid the distractions of envy and find peace in fulfilling our assignments. When we approach our responsibilities with gratitude and diligence, we create a positive atmosphere that inspires others to do the same. This focus strengthens our relationship with God and promotes a positive, supportive environment.

5. Eliminate Comparisons

> *"Comparison is the thief of joy." —Theodore Roosevelt*

It is crucial to avoid making comparisons, as they often breed dissatisfaction. The destructive impact of jealousy on our self-worth is explored in detail in Chapter 2 of this book. When we measure our worth against others, we may foster feelings of inadequacy or envy. Jesus highlighted this principle when he advised his disciples to focus on their individual roles rather than comparing themselves to one another. When Peter inquired about John's future, Jesus replied, *"If it is my will for him to remain until I come, of what concern is that to you? You continue following me." —John 21:22.* Jesus' response reminds us that each person has a unique path and purpose, and our attention should be on fulfilling our own responsibilities rather than evaluating others' roles.

By avoiding comparisons, we can protect ourselves from the trap of jealousy and learn to appreciate our own unique talents and contributions. When we focus on the value of our personal strengths, we cultivate a positive mindset that helps us feel confident and fulfilled, rather than overshadowed by others' accomplishments. This approach allows us to celebrate what we bring to the table, grounding our self-worth in our unique role and purpose rather than in how we measure up to others.

The apostle Paul provided sound counsel:

> *"But let each one examine his own actions, and then he will have reason for rejoicing in regard to himself alone, and not in comparison with the other person." —Galatians 6:4*

The advice in Galatians 6:4 encourages us to evaluate our personal growth and contributions by measuring them against our own progress rather than comparing ourselves to others. By doing so, we can experience genuine joy in our service to God and in fulfilling the unique role He has entrusted to us. This principle is also emphasized in the Parable of the Talents, which illustrates the importance of focusing on faithfully carrying out our responsibilities without comparing them to the assignments given to others. For a deeper exploration of this parable, see how it relates to personal success in Chapter 1 and contentment in Chapter 4.

Romans 12:6-8 beautifully reminds us that we are each uniquely equipped to serve God in our own way when it states, *"We have gifts that differ according to the undeserved kindness given to us."* This scripture emphasizes that Jehovah lovingly grants us different talents and responsibilities suited to our abilities and circumstances. Individual success in each role—whether teaching, encouraging, organizing, or showing kindness—contributes to the overall harmony and unity of the collective.

By avoiding the trap of comparison, we protect our inner peace and inspire others to find joy in their own service, promoting a spirit of unity and mutual respect. Moreover, avoiding comparisons allows us to develop humility and peace of mind in our own lives. When we focus on our own service and unique contributions, we are less likely to harbor jealousy and more likely to find satisfaction in our personal progress and achievements.

From Jealousy To Contentment

Managing jealousy begins with an honest acknowledgment of its presence and a heartfelt desire to overcome it. Recognizing the need for change allows us to take meaningful steps toward aligning our thoughts and actions with God's principles. As we have explored, examining our motives, seeking God's guidance, avoiding comparisons, focusing on our assigned responsibilities, and cultivating gratitude are powerful strategies for transforming feelings of envy into opportunities for growth. These steps promote inner peace and lead to stronger, more meaningful relationships.

A key element in this transformation is humility, which is essential for fostering harmony and guarding our hearts against jealousy. As Chapter 5 highlighted, humility prevents us from provoking jealousy in others by keeping our focus on God's gifts rather than on personal ambition. Similarly, in Chapter 6, humility helps us combat jealousy within ourselves, enabling us to value others' successes without resentment and trust that God's provisions are perfect for each of us. This consistent emphasis on humility across the chapters underscores its role as the anchor that keeps us grounded. The final chapter of this book, Chapter 14, further expands on the superpower of this quality.

By cultivating humility, we strengthen our spiritual growth, relationships, and overall satisfaction. As Proverbs 22:4 reminds us,

> *"The result of humility and the fear of Jehovah is riches and glory and life." —Proverbs 22:4*

When we shift our focus from competition to collaboration and replace resentment with contentment, we reflect the qualities of humility, love, and generosity that God desires in us. Rejoicing in the successes of others and embracing our unique roles frees us from the burden of jealousy, allowing us to find satisfaction in God's provisions. As Proverbs 14:30 wisely states, "A calm heart gives life to the body, but jealousy is rottenness to the bones." Choosing calmness and gratitude leads to spiritual health, inner peace, and lasting joy.

Ultimately, overcoming jealousy is not just about improving our relationships with others—it is also about deepening our relationship with God. Trusting in His timing, purpose, and provision enables us to see our lives through the lens of His love. This transformation cultivates a heart that is at peace. Through this shift, we rid ourselves of jealousy and create an environment of unity, encouragement, and joy that reflects Jehovah's care for all His children.

Chapter 7: Sensitivity To God's Guidance

J ehovah, in His wisdom, provides timely guidance and warnings when jealousy begins to take root. This helps us recognize and address this destructive emotion before it grows. We find such reminders in His Word and sometimes through those close to us, who encourage us to examine our motives and avoid the pitfalls of envy.

Throughout the Bible, we encounter vivid examples of individuals faced with the temptation of jealousy. Some heeded God's counsel, embraced humility, and found peace, while others allowed envy to consume their hearts, leading to tragic consequences. These accounts serve as powerful lessons, showing us the devastating impact of disregarding God's loving warnings and the blessings of listening to His guidance.

One foundational scripture, Philippians 2:3-4, urges us to

> "Do nothing out of contentiousness or out of egotism, but with humility consider others superior to you, as you look out not only for your own interests, but also for the interests of others." —Philippians 2:3-4

This inspired counsel highlights the importance of fostering unity and cooperation. By focusing on the strengths and contributions of others, we can combat feelings of jealousy and cultivate gratitude and mutual respect instead.

In this chapter, we will examine two biblical examples that highlight the dangers of ignoring God's warnings about jealousy. These stories demonstrate how unchecked envy can lead to fractured relationships, spiritual harm, and even physical consequences. As we reflect on these examples, it is beneficial to consider how the practical steps outlined in the preceding chapter could have helped these individuals avoid their unfortunate outcomes. By doing so, we can learn how to safeguard our own hearts and ensure that jealousy never takes root in our lives.

Guidance To Cain

God's interaction with Cain, recounted in Genesis 4:6-7, is an inspiring example of His patience and desire to guide His creation. As discussed in Chapter 3, Cain's story illustrates the destructive potential of jealousy and anger. In this pivotal moment, Jehovah's questions—"Why are you so angry?" and "Why has your countenance fallen?"—invite Cain to reflect on his emotions and take responsibility for his feelings.

Building on that discussion, Chapter 7 emphasizes the timeless relevance of God's counsel. His guiding words, "If you turn to doing good, will you not be restored to favor?" remind us that divine approval is never beyond reach. This lesson closely ties to the principles outlined in Chapter 6, where we explored how self-examination and positive action can redirect negative emotions. God's words encourage us to channel feelings of inadequacy into constructive efforts, focusing on what we can improve rather than dwelling on comparisons with others.

As we live by God's counsel each day, we come to see just how limitless His favor truly is. Like Cain, we can all access God's approval if we humbly examine our motives and strive to do what is right. This approach safeguards our relationship with Him and shield us from the destructive outcomes of envy.

Let's examine God's words closely to glean further insight from them.

Why Are You So Angry?

God's probing question to Cain, *"Why are you so angry?"* (Genesis 4:6), is an invitation to self-reflection. Anger often does not arise in isolation; it is frequently the byproduct of deeper emotions, such as jealousy. In Cain's case, his anger stemmed from his perception that Abel had received God's favor, something Cain deeply desired for himself. However, instead of examining his actions, Cain allowed his jealousy to take root, transforming his inner turmoil into outward hostility and distorting his view of both his brother and Jehovah.

God's question gently redirects Cain's focus inward, encouraging him to consider why he feels this way. It serves as a reminder for us as well: when feelings of jealousy or anger surface, we should pause and ask ourselves, "Why am I feeling this way? Am I focusing on others' success instead of improving my own efforts?" As discussed in Chapter 6, self-examination is a vital first step in overcoming jealousy. By identifying the root cause of our emotions, we can take positive steps to address them.

Why Has Your Countenance Fallen?

God's second question, "Why has your countenance fallen?" (Genesis 4:6), draws attention to how jealousy affects us outwardly. Cain's visible change in demeanor revealed the toll his internal struggles were taking—not just on his relationship with Abel, but also on his own peace of mind. Jealousy often stirs feelings of inadequacy and resentment, creating a cycle of inner conflict that spills over into our interactions with others.

This warning serves as an important reminder: jealousy does not resolve itself. Instead, it grows, reshaping our thoughts, influencing our decisions, and eventually leading to actions we may deeply regret. The practical strategies in Chapter 5, such as cultivating humility and focusing on gratitude, help us prevent jealousy from taking root and protect our relationships with others and Jehovah.

In modern times, we see how the internal struggles of jealousy, much like Cain's, can profoundly affect mental health and social interactions. Jealousy can foster chronic stress, anxiety, and even depression as individuals constantly compare themselves to others. Social media has amplified this phenomenon, often creating a false sense of inadequacy and fueling envy. Just as Cain's countenance visibly reflected his inner turmoil, today, jealousy often manifests outwardly in strained relationships, avoidance, or passive-aggressive behaviors.

Understanding these effects reminds us of the importance of addressing jealousy early. Practical steps, such as cultivating humility and gratitude (discussed in Chapter 5), help mitigate jealousy's destructive impact. Additionally, engaging in open communication with trusted friends or loved ones can help diffuse misunderstandings and rebuild trust. These measures preserve relationships and promote mental and emotional well-being, ensuring that jealousy does not take root and rob us of inner peace.

Turn To Doing Good

God's counsel to Cain, *"If you turn to doing good, will you not be restored to favor?"* (Genesis 4:7), serves as a profound reminder of His mercy and love. It emphasizes that God's approval is not determined by past mistakes but is based entirely on our choices and sincere efforts to correct our paths. Cain's situation was not irreversible; God's favor was not a limited resource reserved for Abel alone. Cain had the same opportunity to gain God's approval if he chose to adjust his actions and attitude.

By framing the solution as "doing good," Jehovah gently guided Cain to focus his energy on positive, constructive actions rather than allowing jealousy to control him. This timeless principle reminds us that favor with God is not a prize to be won through rivalry or competition. Instead, it is available to all who approach Him with sincere hearts and strive to do what is right.

This counsel remains just as relevant today. When we feel overshadowed by others' successes, it is vital to remember that God's blessings are abundant and tailored to each individual's unique circumstances. Instead of comparing ourselves to others, we can choose humility, which allows us to focus on personal growth and self-improvement. As discussed in Chapter 5, this shift in perspective helps us avoid the destructive cycle of jealousy.

When we align our actions with God's guidance, we experience profound peace and joy, knowing that we are pleasing Him. This reassurance strengthens our trust in His love and reminds us that He values our individual efforts, regardless of where we stand in relation to others. God's blessings, like His love, are limitless, and embracing this truth can free us from feelings of inadequacy or envy.

Guidance To The Older Sibling

In Jesus' parable of the prodigal son (Luke 15:11-32), the older brother serves as a vivid example of how jealousy and resentment can take root, even in someone who is outwardly faithful. This account emphasizes that jealousy is not confined to material things; it often extends to emotional matters, such as love, affection, and perceived fairness. The older brother felt overshadowed by the celebration for his sibling, believing his father had overlooked his years of loyalty.

His bitter words, "Look! These many years I have slaved for you and never disobeyed your orders," reveal a deep longing for recognition and validation (Luke 15:29). This mirrors the underlying struggles discussed in Chapter 5, where humility is highlighted as essential in navigating jealousy. The father's calm and loving response to his son, "My son, you have always been with me, and all that is mine is yours" (Luke 15:31), echoes the principle in Chapter 5 that humility enables us to appreciate our own blessings instead of measuring our worth against that of others.

The older brother's reaction shows how a lack of humility can fuel jealousy, even in relationships where love and blessings are already present. As Chapter 5 explains, cultivating humility involves redirecting our attention away from feelings of entitlement and toward gratitude for what we have. This attitude helps us maintain peace and prevents unnecessary resentment, even when others receive attention or praise.

All Things That Are Mine Are Yours

The older brother's struggle was not with material loss but with emotional validation. His bitter words to his father revealed a deep-seated feeling of being overlooked and unappreciated. He perceived his loyalty as going unnoticed, while his younger brother received celebration and attention. In response, the father lovingly reassured him that everything he possessed belonged to him as well.

This interaction underscores how jealousy often arises—not from an actual lack, but from the perception that someone else's gain diminishes our own value or standing. It is not the blessings themselves that fuel jealousy, but the belief that they come at our expense. The older brother saw the father's joy for the prodigal son as a reflection of his own worth being diminished, rather than recognizing the constancy of his father's love for him.

The father's tender response reminds us that, rather than comparing ourselves to others, we should reflect on the blessings we already enjoy. As discussed in Chapter 6, cultivating gratitude can help us recognize the consistent love and care that Jehovah provides. By focusing on these blessings, we can free ourselves from feelings of inadequacy or resentment, finding peace in the knowledge that we are deeply valued by Him.

Embracing Compassion Over A Sense of Fairness

The father's invitation to the older brother to share in the joy of his sibling's return reveals a vital principle that compassion and forgiveness should outweigh any notion of personal entitlement. The father chose not to dwell on the prodigal son's past mistakes but to focus on the restored relationship, showing that true joy comes from reconciliation and unity. This reflects God's perspective—He delights in unity and reconciliation, not in keeping score.

Compassion and forgiveness bring profound benefits to the recipient and to the giver. They free the giver from the burdens of jealousy, including bitterness and resentment. The father's example demonstrates that choosing love over entitlement leads to deeper satisfaction and lasting peace. By inviting the older brother to join the celebration, the father offers more than a chance to participate in the festivities—he extends an opportunity to let go of jealousy and embrace the joy of family restoration.

This lesson closely aligns with the principles of humility and love outlined in Chapter 5. Focusing on empathy in place of entitlement enables us to celebrate the achievements and fortunes of others, preventing the rifts that envy frequently fosters. The father's gentle reasoning challenges us to rise above personal grievances and adopt a broader perspective of love and unity.

The father's response to the older brother touches on a powerful theme that often intersects with jealousy: the perception of fairness. The older brother's bitterness stemmed not from the loss of possessions but from his conviction that his father's decisions were unfair—that celebrating the prodigal son diminished the recognition he deserved for his own loyalty. This struggle with fairness mirrors the feelings expressed by the vineyard workers in Jesus' parable (Matthew 20:1-16), where the landowner's generosity toward latecomers stirred envy among those who had labored all day.

These narratives challenge our understanding of fairness by highlighting God's impartial generosity. As individuals, we often perceive fairness as absolute equality, assessing our own resources against those allotted to others. However, Jehovah's perspective is different. He considers individual needs, circumstances, and efforts, tailoring His blessings perfectly to each person. By trusting in His wisdom, we can learn to rise above jealousy and embrace gratitude, knowing that His provision is always just and sufficient.

Chapter 8 delves deeper into the complex relationship between fairness and jealousy, exploring how these feelings can cloud our perspective and hinder our ability to rejoice in others' blessings. By understanding God's abundant love and impartiality, we can replace feelings of rivalry with compassion and contentment, cultivating unity and joy in our relationships. This shift in focus enables us to experience the profound joy that comes from fostering peace and mutual understanding, strengthening our bonds with others, and deepening our relationship with Jehovah.

Lessons From Cain And The Prodigal Son

The accounts of Cain and the prodigal son's older brother offer profound lessons about the destructive nature of jealousy and the importance of overcoming it. In Genesis 4:7 God told Cain: *"if you do not turn to doing good, sin is crouching at the door, and its craving is to dominate you."* This paints a vivid picture of how sin actively seeks to dominate us, especially when brought about by jealousy. This imagery reminds us that jealousy is not a passive emotion—it grows and intensifies if we fail to address it, potentially leading to devastating consequences. However, God's assurance to Cain that he could *"conquer it"* indicates that with God's help, overcoming harmful emotions is always possible.

Both accounts highlight the importance of introspection and personal accountability. Jehovah's counsel to Cain, *"If you turn to doing good, will you not be restored to favor?"* (Genesis 4:7), serves as a powerful reminder of the transformative impact of self-reflection and positive action. Similarly, the father's gentle reasoning with the older brother in Jesus' parable encourages us to examine our own attitudes and motives. These invitations to reflect and make the necessary adjustments to correct a wrong course align closely with the principles of self-examination discussed in Chapter 6.

Together, these inspired examples demonstrate that identifying and addressing the root causes of jealousy—whether feelings of inadequacy, pride, or comparison—enables us to realign our thoughts and actions with God's way of thinking. From Cain's tragic example, we learn the importance of heeding God's loving counsel before jealousy grows into anger and leads to actions we may deeply regret. Likewise, from the older brother's struggle, we learn to guard against emotional jealousy by focusing on gratitude and trust in God's fairness and love.

By replacing jealousy with gratitude, humility, and love, we protect our inner peace and preserve the harmony of our relationships. The father's invitation to the older brother to join the celebration of the prodigal son's return reflects a godly perspective—one that prioritizes reconciliation, compassion, and joy over a rigid sense of fairness. This perspective reminds us that favor with Jehovah is not a competition but a reflection of our sincere efforts to do good and remain faithful.

God's guidance, both in ancient times and today, provides the tools we need to resist this destructive emotion called jealousy. Through His Word, sincere and loving counsel from others, and the reassurance of His mercy, we are empowered to *"turn to doing good"* and experience the blessings and success that come from His approval. When we choose to follow His guidance, we strengthen our relationship with Him and reflect His boundless love in our interactions with others, thereby cultivating peace in our hearts.

> *"Wise men learn more from fools than fools from the wise."*
> *—Marcus Aurelius*

Marcus Aurelius's observation proves true regarding the accounts of Cain and the prodigal son's older brother. The stories provide a compelling contrast, illustrating the spectrum of jealousy—from destructive outward actions to internalized resentment. By examining these accounts side by side, we gain a fuller understanding of how jealousy can manifest and the importance of addressing it at its root.

Cain represents the extreme end of the spectrum, where jealousy grows into bitterness and ultimately leads to violent actions. Instead of redirecting his emotions, Cain allowed his jealousy to fester, leading to murder. His actions serve as a sobering reminder of how envy, when acted upon, can fracture relationships and result in irreversible harm.

On the other hand, the older brother illustrates a more subtle yet equally harmful form of jealousy—internalized resentment. This hidden resentment poisons his view of his family and blinds him to the blessings he already enjoys, such as his father's unwavering love and the security of his inheritance.

While Cain's jealousy was explosive and outwardly destructive, the older brother's envy was inward, festering as bitterness that robbed him of joy. Both cases reveal that jealousy, whether acted upon or internalized, can severely damage relationships and hinder spiritual growth.

These contrasting examples teach us important lessons about jealousy:

1. *Self-Reflection*: Cain ignored Jehovah's warning to examine his motives, while the older brother resisted his father's invitation to reflect on his blessings. Both stories underscore the need for introspection as a defense against jealousy.

2. *Gratitude*: Focusing on our blessings—such as the older brother's security in his father's house—can prevent feelings of inadequacy and resentment.

3. *Action vs. Inaction*: Cain's story warns us of the dangers of acting on jealous impulses, while the older brother's tale highlights the harm of harboring jealousy without addressing it.

Ultimately, these accounts remind us that jealousy, whether overt or hidden, requires proactive steps to overcome. By cultivating humility, gratitude, and trust in Jehovah's impartial love, we can break free from jealousy's grip and preserve our inner peace and relationships.

Chapter 8: The Link Between Jealousy And Fairness

As explored in Chapter 7, God's guidance invites us to confront jealousy with humility and reflection. Building on this, the father's invitation to the older brother in the Parable of the Prodigal Son (Luke 15:25-32) highlights the transformative power of compassion over fairness. This chapter delves into the link between jealousy and fairness, challenging us to rise above human perceptions of fairness and embrace Jehovah's impartial generosity.

Jesus' Parable of the Vineyard Workers in Matthew 20:1-16 expands on this theme, demonstrating how jealousy can arise when blessings are perceived to be distributed unequally. In the account, a landowner hires workers at various times throughout the day. At the end of the day, he pays each worker the same agreed-upon wage, regardless of how many hours they worked. Those hired early in the day feel slighted, saying:

> "These last men put in one hour's work; still you made them equal to us who bore the burden of the day and the burning heat!" —Matthew 20:12

The landowner patiently responds:

> "Fellow, I do you no wrong. You agreed with me for a denarius, did you not? Take what is yours and go. I want to give to this last one the same as to you. Do I not have the right to do what I want with my own things? Or is your eye envious because I am good?" —Matthew 20:13-15

This parable closely mirrors the feelings of the older brother in the story of the Prodigal Son. Both the vineyard workers and the older brother grappled with jealousy, rooted in the belief that others have received generosity they do not deserve. This jealousy often stems from a distorted perception of fairness—a belief that others should not receive or possess more than we do, whether it be authority, wealth, recognition, or happiness.

In these moments, the default tendency is not to rejoice in another person's blessing but to demand restitution—either by insisting on receiving more for ourselves or, even worse, by demanding that what the other person has received be taken away. This attitude clouds our perception of the giver's generosity and blinds us to the abundance of our own blessings. Instead, our subconscious fixates on "equalizing" the situation, leaving us restless and dissatisfied until we feel the perceived imbalance has been restored.

This mindset reflects a scarcity mentality—the flawed belief that blessings are finite and that someone else's gain diminishes our own. Such thinking fosters resentment and prevents us from sharing in the joy of others. By focusing on comparisons rather than contentment, we forfeit the peace and gratitude that come from appreciating our own blessings.

The vineyard workers' jealousy stems from their belief that the landowner's generosity toward the later workers somehow diminished their own reward. However, the scarcity trap in which they were caught ignored the fact that their needs were fully met—they received exactly what was promised. Similarly, when we view life's blessings as limited, we risk falling into the same trap. This compromised perspective can lead us to feel as though we've been deprived whenever others are blessed.

Just as the father in the Prodigal Son parable extended love and reconciliation to both his sons, the landowner in the Vineyard Workers parable invites us to trust in the fairness of the giver rather than the perception of fairness through human eyes. The older brother's reaction mirrors the workers' feelings of indignation over perceived inequality: "Why should someone who worked only one hour receive the same wage as we who toiled all day?"

In contrast, an abundance mentality recognizes Jehovah's limitless provision. His blessings are impartial and perfectly suited to each individual. These accounts challenge us to look beyond strict equality and to see God's impartial generosity. As Psalm 145:16 reminds us:

> "You open your hand and satisfy the desire of every living thing." —Psalm 145:16

The landowner's generosity was not a subtraction from the earlier workers' reward but an expression of his kindness. Likewise, God's consideration of others does not diminish His care for us. These parables challenge us to cultivate trust in God's wisdom when we feel overlooked or undervalued. By meditating on His generosity, we can shift our perspective and appreciate the unique ways in which God satisfies all our needs.

Finding Peace In God's Perfect Justice

Hannah's experience in the Bible book of 1 Samuel provides a profound lesson in trusting God's impartiality and embracing His timing. For years, she endured the emotional pain of barrenness and the taunts of her rival, Peninnah (1 Samuel 1:6-7). Yet, instead of allowing bitterness or feelings of unfairness to consume her, Hannah turned to Jehovah in heartfelt prayer. Her response demonstrates a crucial principle: rather than focusing on the perceived advantage of others, we can find peace in knowing that God's care is both impartial and perfectly timed.

God's impartiality is evident in how He answered Hannah's prayer, not simply by blessing her with a child but by providing her with a role of lasting significance as the mother of Samuel, a prophet and leader in Israel. God did not overlook Hannah's tears or her devotion. Her joyful prayer after Samuel's birth reflects her understanding of God's justice: "He raises the lowly one from the dust; He lifts up the poor from the ash heap" (1 Samuel 2:8). By meditating on God's fairness and focusing on gratitude, Hannah found peace and avoided the bitterness that envy can produce.

Hannah's experience illustrates that God's blessings are not allocated according to human standards of fairness. Instead, He lovingly supplies what we need according to His perfect will. When we trust in His impartiality, we can release feelings of resentment and rejoice in His provision for others, confident that He sees and cares for us as well.

When tempted to compare your circumstances with others, follow Hannah's example by turning to Jehovah in prayer. Reflect on His perfect justice and abundant love, trusting that His blessings for you are uniquely suited to your needs. This mindset fosters contentment and strengthens your bond with Him.

Life Is Not A Zero-Sum Game

The Parable of the Vineyard Workers emphasizes that blessings are not distributed on a first-come, first-served basis, but rather according to the generous will of the giver. Similarly, the father's interaction with the older brother in Jesus' Parable of the Prodigal Son reinforces the principle that life is not a zero-sum game in which one person's gain diminishes another's. Instead, God's blessings reflect His boundless love, which is abundant enough to provide for all.

This theme is echoed in God's loving counsel to Cain in Genesis 4:6-7. Tragically, Cain allowed jealousy to fester, leading to devastating consequences. By contrast, the older brother in the parable is left standing at a crossroads. Though frustrated by what he perceives as an injustice, he has the opportunity to reflect on his father's heartfelt invitation: "*Son, you have always been with me, and all the things that are mine are yours.*" (Luke 15:31) The father's words remind the older brother that he has never lacked anything and that his father's joy in welcoming the younger son does not diminish his own inheritance. Marcus Aurelius beautifully captured this thought when he said,

> "*The joy of one does not subtract from the joy of another; in fact, shared joy only multiplies.*" —Marcus Aurelius

By leaving the response of the older brother open-ended in the Parable of the Prodigal Son, Jesus invites his listeners—and, by extension, all of us—to reflect on our attitudes. Would we, like the older brother, resist sharing in someone else's joy, potentially risking the disastrous outcome experienced by Cain? Or would we choose to embrace a forgiving and generous spirit, as exemplified by the father? This reflection challenges us to consider how we respond when others receive blessings that we feel they may not deserve.

Such reflection is vital for overcoming jealousy. When we shift our focus from comparison to thankfulness, we free ourselves from the emotional weight of envy. We begin to see that Jehovah's blessings are not distributed unfairly but lovingly, according to His wisdom. By trusting in His love, we can align our hearts with His and find joy in unity and restoration rather than in division and resentment.

It is easy to see why the zero-sum mentality is so deeply rooted in society. In today's competitive world, slogans like "He Who Dies with The Most Toys Wins" perpetuate the belief that there can only be one winner. This perspective influences various aspects of life. From an early age, we are often taught— whether explicitly or implicitly—that success is a limited resource and that we must strive to "win" at all costs.

In school, grades are ranked, awards are given to the top performers, and recognition is reserved for those who outshine their peers. Similarly, in sports, emphasis is frequently placed on the importance of victory, with slogans like "second place is just the first loser" perpetuating the idea that anything less than being at the top is a failure.

This mindset fosters a zero-sum view of life, where one person's success is automatically seen as another's loss. It creates an unhealthy pressure to constantly measure ourselves against others, leading to feelings of inadequacy when we don't come out on top. Over time, this way of thinking can overshadow the value of personal growth, collaboration, and shared success. It may also hinder us from celebrating the achievements of others, as doing so can feel like acknow- ledging our own perceived shortcomings—a reminder that we are merely the "first loser."

Ultimately, life is not a race where there can only be one winner. Instead, it's an opportunity to grow, collaborate, and support one another, knowing that God's love and blessings are abundant enough for all. Each of us has a unique path to follow, as the apostle Paul reminds us,

> "Let us run with endurance the race that is set before us." —
> Hebrews 12:1

This perspective encourages us to focus on our personal efforts, achievements and progress rather than comparing ourselves to others. By challenging the zero-sum mentality, we can replace feelings of rivalry with joy in both our own accomplishments and those of others.

Cultivating An Abundance Mentality

The landowner's rhetorical question, "Is *your eye envious because I am good?*" (Matthew 20:15), mirrors Jehovah's probing questions to Cain in Genesis 4:6-7: "*Why are you so angry, and why has your countenance fallen?*" Both accounts encourage deep self-reflection and a willingness to look beyond the immediate emotions of envy or injustice. The vineyard workers, like Cain and the older brother in the Parable of the Prodigal Son, were invited to realign their perspectives—to view blessings for others not as a loss to themselves but as a reflection of the giver's goodness and generosity.

Developing an abundance mentality begins with this same realignment of focus. It requires us to see life not as a competition for limited resources but as an opportunity to trust in God's limitless love and care. God's blessings are not rationed or distributed based on human calculations of fairness; they flow abundantly, as perfectly measured gifts tailored to meet our needs.

When we meditate on God's generosity, our perspectives shift. Rather than comparing ourselves to others, we learn to appreciate the unique ways in which God takes care of each individual. The Bible reminds us of this reality, assuring us that,

> "[Jehovah can] *do more than superabundantly beyond all the things we ask or conceive.*" —Ephesians 3:20

An abundance mentality flourishes when we actively cultivate gratitude, as King David consistently demonstrated throughout his life. By regularly reflecting on God's blessings—both spiritual and material—David uprooted feelings of jealousy and replaced them with appreciation. In Psalm 103:2, David wrote: *"Let me praise Jehovah; May I never forget all that He has done."* This heartfelt expression captures the essence of David's relationship with God—a life characterized by a constant recognition of God's goodness.

Even during times of trial, such as when he fled from Saul or faced family challenges, David turned to God in prayer, expressing gratitude for His care and asking for strength. This habit of prayerful gratitude deepened David's trust in God and enabled him to see God's hand clearly in his life.

Furthermore, David exemplified an abundance mentality by rejoicing in the blessings of others and acknowledging God's goodness in their lives. For instance, when David prepared for the temple's construction, he willingly celebrated the generosity of those who contributed, seeing it as evidence of God's abundant provision (1 Chronicles 29:9-14). This perspective cultivated harmony and fulfillment, enhancing both David's experiences and the lives of those he guided.

An abundance mentality is rooted in trust—trust in God's limitless provision and His deep understanding of our needs. How can we cultivate this mindset in our daily lives?

1. *Reflect on God's Past Provision:* Take time to recall specific ways Jehovah has cared for you. Psalm 37:25 assures us: *"I was once young and now I am old, but I have not seen anyone righteous abandoned, nor his children looking for bread."* Reflecting on these provisions builds confidence in God's ability to provide abundantly.

2. *Practice Gratitude Daily:* Each day, write down one thing for which you are thankful, whether small or significant. This practice can help you focus on God's generosity rather than comparing yourself to others. As 1 Thessalonians 5:18 encourages, *"Give thanks for everything. This is God's will for you in Christ Jesus."*

3. *Pray for Contentment:* Regularly ask God for peace of mind and a joyful heart. Proverbs 30:8-9 reminds us to seek balance and trust: *"[...] Give me neither poverty nor riches. Just let me consume my portion of food."*

Through recognizing God's unwavering care, fostering an attitude of thankfulness, and seeking peace through prayer, we can develop a mindset of abundance and embrace the tranquility found in God's perfect provision.

I Will Lack Nothing

Ultimately, the lessons of these parables remind us that God's love and mercy extend to everyone—whether it is the repentant prodigal, the faithful older brother, or even someone like Cain, who was given the opportunity to change but chose not to. God's compassion assures us that letting go of jealousy and trusting in His promises leads to greater joy, unity, and peace.

The accounts of Cain, the Parable of the Prodigal Son, and the Parable of the Vineyard Workers serve as compassionate warnings and invaluable guides for mastering jealousy. Rather than outright condemning the protagonists in these stories, Jehovah grants them opportunities to reflect, adjust their perspectives, and take positive steps to correct their thinking. These accounts remind us that emotions such as jealousy may arise naturally, but they do not have to control or define us. By examining our motives, focusing on constructive actions, and aligning our thoughts with God's, we can overcome envy and cultivate a heart of love.

If placed in the shoes of the older brother or the early vineyard workers, how would we respond? Would we allow feelings of jealousy and perceived unfairness to rob us of joy? Or would we follow the advice of the father in the Parable of the Prodigal Son and choose to embrace a forgiving and generous spirit, finding satisfaction in the blessings we already enjoy? These reflections challenge us to shift our focus from comparison to humility and gratitude, thereby fostering trust in God's boundless care.

The parables, in particular, challenge our view of fairness. By embracing an abundance mentality, we can rejoice in the blessings of others, confident that God's care for us is equally abundant and uniquely suited to our circumstances. This perspective helps us to share in the joy of others while deepening our trust in God's unchanging goodness. In doing so, we align ourselves with His purpose and foster unity, joy, and peace.

God's loving guidance acts as signposts that steer us away from jealousy and toward gratitude and trust in His fairness and generosity. When we feel that life is unfair, gratitude becomes a powerful antidote to jealousy rooted in perceived inequities. For a deeper discussion of the role gratitude and self-reflection play in spiritual growth, see Chapter 6.

King David demonstrated his unwavering trust in God's ability to provide for all his needs by maintaining an attitude of gratitude. This gratitude created a virtuous cycle—David's appreciation for what he had led to even greater blessings from God.

God abundantly blessed David, as David himself declared:

> *"Jehovah is my Shepherd. I will lack nothing." —Psalm 23:1*

Ultimately, developing an abundance mentality reflects our trust in Jehovah's power to care for us fully. When we view life through this lens, we avoid jealousy and focus on the enduring blessings we already enjoy. This helps us recognize that others' success is evidence of God's goodness. Like David, we can confidently rest in God's boundless care, assured that His provisions are always more than sufficient for all our needs.

As we have seen, the concept of fairness can become a battleground for jealousy when viewed through a human lens. In Chapter 9, we will explore how this dynamic intensifies within close relationships, where personal history and biases come into play.

Chapter 9: Familiarity Breeds Contempt

J ealousy becomes particularly potent and destructive when directed toward someone the aggressor knows well, especially when the aggressor believes that the person does not deserve success or should not surpass them. This proximity magnifies the sting of the target's achievements, making them harder for the aggressor to accept. The familiarity between the two sharpens feelings of envy, as the aggressor perceives themselves as having a clearer view of the target's flaws, weaknesses, or perceived unworthiness.

> *"Great men, unknown in their villages, are famous in the world." —Chinese proverb*

The above Chinese proverb wisely highlights how familiarity, which once cultivated companionship and comfort, can quickly turn into a source of contempt when success enters the equation. Knowing the individual's history—their past mistakes, vulnerabilities, and imperfections—creates a frustrating contradiction for the aggressor. While the world celebrates this person's rise, the aggressor cannot reconcile how someone they have underestimated or even looked down upon could achieve such prominence.

This tension fuels confusion, frustration, and eventually bitterness. Intimate knowledge, which could inspire a sense of pride in the other's achievements, instead amplifies feelings of inadequacy and resentment. The aggressor's perspective is clouded by their personal history with the individual, making it impossible to see the celebrated figure others now respect and admire. What remains is a festering bitterness, born of a warped familiarity that has soured into scorn.

This truth is vividly demonstrated in the Bible, where even those closest to great figures like Moses and Jesus struggled to see beyond their own jealousy. Their stories remind us that envy thrives within the intimacy of close relationships.

Jesus Faced Envy's Sting From Loved Ones

Jesus mentioned that *"a prophet is not without honor except in his home territory and in his own house"* (Matthew 13:57). When he returned to Nazareth, the people there struggled to accept him as the Messiah because they knew him as the carpenter's son, someone they had watched grow up in their midst. Their familiarity with his earthly family and background blinded them to his divine identity and mission. They couldn't reconcile the image of the humble carpenter's son with the role of the promised Messiah, and as a result, they lacked faith in him.

This inability to see Jesus for who he truly was reflects how familiarity can lead people to undervalue or misjudge others, overlooking the unique qualities or gifts they may possess. Just as those in his hometown failed to recognize his divine role, individuals who harbor jealousy toward someone close to them often overlook the qualities or blessings that Jehovah has bestowed upon that person.

Even Jesus' own brothers struggled to accept his growing prominence and the unique role he had been given. Their familiarity with him as a sibling, someone they had grown up with, clouded their ability to recognize his divine purpose. In John 7:3-5, they said to him: *"Leave here and go into Judea, so that your disciples may also see the works you are doing."* They suggested that he leave for another town under the pretense of offering help, implying that he needed to demonstrate his abilities elsewhere to gain greater recognition. Yet, their words revealed a deeper issue: *"His brothers were, in fact, not exercising faith in him"* (John 7:5).

The suggestion to leave was not rooted in genuine support or admiration but in an underlying discomfort with his growing influence. They could not stand the idea of constantly being reminded of his achievements, perhaps feeling overshadowed by his spiritual mission and the attention he garnered. The tension between their familial familiarity and Jesus' divine role created a barrier to their faith in him. Rather than celebrating his works and mission, they distanced themselves emotionally, masking their discomfort with what appeared to be practical advice.

Their advice that he move on was not motivated by concern for his best interests but by a desire to alleviate their own discomfort. His continued presence and witnessing the reverence others had for him likely served as a constant reminder of their struggle to accept his unique identity and purpose. This account underscores how even the closest relationships can become strained when familiarity prevents appreciation for someone's true worth.

Their behavior also illustrates that, no matter how hard you try to avoid provoking jealousy in others, you may still fall short. Jealousy is not always a response to someone's behavior; it often stems from struggles within the individual experiencing it. Jesus never acted in a way that was boastful or dismissive of others, including his own siblings. Being perfect, he exemplified love, humility, and respect in all his interactions. Yet, despite his flawless conduct and his consistent efforts to treat them with kindness and dignity, his brothers still harbored negative feelings toward him.

This illustrates that jealousy is not necessarily caused by wrongdoing on the part of the one envied but can arise from the insecurities, misunderstandings, or pride of the observer. Jesus' siblings likely felt overshadowed by his growing prominence and struggled with their inability to understand his divine purpose. Their familiarity with him as a brother—the boy with whom they had grown up—made it hard to reconcile the image of a Messiah performing miracles and drawing crowds of followers. Their internal conflicts, not anything he did, probably contributed to their feelings of discomfort and jealousy.

This account shows that even our best efforts to avoid provoking jealousy in others may not protect us from their envy. It is not always within our power to control how others perceive or react to our achievements or qualities, no matter how well-intentioned we may be. However, the strategies outlined in Chapter 5 are still relevant, as Jesus' example teaches us to remain patient and steadfast in our purpose, regardless of how others respond. He did not let his brothers' lack of faith deter him from his mission, nor did he compromise his integrity to gain their approval. Instead, he continued to show love and remained focused on fulfilling his assignment to the best of his ability, trusting that time and truth would eventually be on his side.

Ultimately, this serves as encouragement for us. If even the Son of God, a perfect man, faced jealousy and misunderstanding, we should not be disheartened when we encounter similar challenges. What matters most is staying true to our values and maintaining a loving, humble disposition, just as Jesus did.

Moses Faced Envy's Sting From Loved Ones

Another example from the Bible is found in the story of Moses and his siblings, Aaron and Miriam. Jehovah chose Moses to lead the Israelites out of Egypt and granted him the unique privilege of speaking to Him *"face to face,"* (Numbers 12:6-8). However, Aaron and Miriam struggled to accept his elevated role, possibly due to their familiarity with him as their brother and their awareness of his shortcomings.

Moses openly acknowledged his struggle with speaking. When Jehovah first commissioned him to lead the Israelites out of Egypt, Moses humbly admitted: *"I have never been a fluent speaker... for I am slow of speech and slow of tongue"* (Exodus 4:10). In response, Jehovah allowed Aaron to serve as Moses' spokesman before Pharaoh. The siblings might have reasoned that Moses was not naturally equipped for such an important role or that they were more deserving of it.

In Numbers 12:1-2, we read that Aaron and Miriam spoke against Moses, questioning his authority and expressing jealousy. They asked, *"Is it only through Moses that Jehovah has spoken? Has he not also spoken through us?"* Their jealousy led them to overlook Moses' unique relationship with God and the special role he was given. Instead of appreciating Moses's leadership, they allowed their closeness to cloud their respect for him, questioning why he should be favored above them.

Similar to the case of Jesus, this account illustrates how familiarity can breed jealousy and compromise one's perception of another's qualities and divinely appointed role. Aaron and Miriam's inability to see Moses as more than their brother led them to question his authority. Just as the people in Nazareth couldn't recognize Jesus as the Messiah because they only knew him as the carpenter's son, Aaron and Miriam's familiarity with Moses as their sibling prevented them from acknowledging the unique blessings God had bestowed upon him as the leader of Israel.

As with Jesus, Moses exemplified humility, consistently demonstrating a desire for others to succeed and share in the blessings of God's service. Despite being chosen for a unique role, Moses never exerted authority over others or sought personal glory. Instead, he exhibited a selfless leadership style, often prioritizing the needs of others above his own and seeking their spiritual and physical well-being. However, even Moses' humility and generous spirit did not shield him from the jealousy of those closest to him.

Beyond The Boundaries Of Human Thinking

> *"'For my thoughts are not your thoughts, and your ways are not my ways,' declares Jehovah. 'For as the heavens are higher than the earth, so my ways are higher than your ways and my thoughts than your thoughts.'"* —Isaiah 55:8-9

These examples show how familiarity can obscure the gifts, roles, or blessings that God bestows upon others. The aggressor, convinced of their own view of the target's supposed flaws, may struggle to understand how someone so familiar and so "ordinary" in their eyes could experience success. They fail to recognize that the success they are witnessing is not merely the result of the target's personal abilities or circumstances, but is, in fact, a reflection of God's blessing. God's invisible hand often works in ways that defy human understanding, and those consumed by jealousy fail to see this divine intervention. Instead of acknowledging that God rewards faithfulness, diligence, and integrity, the aggressor focuses solely on the visible aspects of the target's success—

status, accomplishments, recognition—while completely missing the spiritual foundation that underpins it.

This blindness to God's role in the observable outcomes exacerbates the aggressor's jealousy. They may believe that success is to be earned through worldly measures—power, influence, or manipulation. When someone succeeds, despite not following worldly strategies, especially someone others believe should not outshine them, it creates a deep internal conflict. The aggressor is confused and frustrated because their understanding of success is based on their own limited view of fairness and merit. They cannot comprehend how the person they look down upon could be experiencing favor and prosperity, failing to grasp Jehovah's hand in such matters.

This was especially evident in the story of Joseph. His brothers struggled to comprehend why Joseph, the younger sibling, should receive special dreams. To them, Joseph had no right to surpass his older siblings in stature or favor. How could someone so familiar, someone they had known all their lives, be destined for such greatness? They refused to see that Jehovah had a purpose for Joseph, a purpose that was beyond their understanding. Instead of respecting that purpose, their jealousy blinded them to the divine plan at work, and they plotted to remove Joseph from the equation entirely. They could not perceive the invisible hand of God guiding Joseph's life and blessing him for his faithfulness.

Saul's jealousy of David followed a similar pattern. Saul, as king, knew David well. He had seen David grow up in his court, witnessed his victories on the battlefield, and even benefited from David's loyalty and service. Yet, when David's success began to eclipse Saul's, the king could not accept it. In Saul's eyes, David was not supposed to surpass him; David was supposed to remain subordinate. Saul's jealousy became so intense that he could not recognize that God's hand was behind David's blessings. David's victories, popularity, and rise to prominence were not mere coincidences or results of personal ambition—they were signs of God's favor and blessing. However, Saul, blinded by his own pride and envy, could not see this. Instead of understanding that God was working through David for the good of Israel, Saul viewed David's achievements as a personal affront and a threat to his own power.

In all these cases, the aggressors were close to the targets of their envy—they knew them intimately, and this familiarity made the success of their targets all the more intolerable. Their jealousy was rooted in a false sense of superiority or entitlement, believing that they, not the target, deserved to succeed. They failed to see God's hand behind the blessings of their targets. The aggressors were so consumed by their own envy and confusion that they missed the spiritual reality: Jehovah provides success to those who are faithful to Him, and His favor cannot be earned or predicted by worldly standards.

Closeness can cause people to undervalue or misjudge others, overlooking the unique qualities or talents they may possess. Furthermore, human expectations do not determine success. Rather than focusing on others' achievements with envy, it is essential to recognize that true success comes from aligning oneself with God's will and trusting in His guidance. Only by doing so can one truly understand and appreciate the blessings of those around them, rather than allowing jealousy to take root and skew their perception.

A Tale of Friendship and Jealousy

A good friend, we'll call him Jack, once shared a fascinating story with me about the subtle nature of envy. When he was in college, he started dating a young woman we'll call Jill. Their budding relationship seemed to bring them both a lot of joy. However, a friend of Jack's, let's call him John, began to question Jack about his choice. John casually remarked that Jill wasn't particularly attractive and suggested that Jack could "do much better."

Initially, Jack brushed off John's comments as nothing more than friendly banter. After all, the two often joked around together. However, as time went on, Jack began to dwell on John's words. The more he thought about it, the more he started to question his feelings for Jill. Eventually, Jack ended the relationship, even feeling grateful to John for what he believed was genuine advice.

Of course, not long afterward, John began dating Jill himself.

While the details of this story may vary, it's easy to see how situations like these could unfold in different settings—whether among friends at school, colleagues at work, or within social circles. It shows how envy and ulterior motives can hide behind seemingly harmless words, subtly influencing decisions and relationships.

John's seemingly casual remarks about Jill disguised his hidden envy toward Jack's relationship. Under the guise of friendly concern, John sowed seeds of doubt in Jack's mind, subtly undermining his friend's happiness. The true depth of John's envy was revealed when he began dating Jill himself.

This story underscores how those who are closest to us are often the most vulnerable to feelings of envy. The closeness of their bond, instead of fostering trust and support, became a breeding ground for rivalry and subtle betrayal. John's envy corroded his ability to genuinely celebrate his friend's happiness, leading to manipulative behavior that fractured their relationship.

You Will Face Envy's Sting From Loved Ones

"History might not repeat itself, but it does rhyme." —Mark Twain

Given these examples, it is very likely that you, too, will encounter jealousy from those closest to you, including members of your own family. Familiarity, as we have seen, can sometimes lead to a distorted view of someone's qualities, blessings, or achievements, making it difficult for others to fully appreciate what Jehovah has done in their lives. However, armed with the knowledge we have gained from these Biblical accounts, we are better equipped to respond with understanding, patience, and love. Rather than allowing jealousy to create division, we can view these moments as opportunities to support our loved ones by showing patience, empathy, and understanding as they work through their emotions.

It is essential to remember that envy often stems from deep-seated insecurities or misunderstandings rather than intentional malice. Just as Cain, Joseph's brothers, and Saul allowed their feelings of inadequacy to cloud their perspective, those close to us may similarly struggle to process their emotions in a healthy way. By acknowledging their struggles and avoiding defensive or retaliatory reactions, we can imitate the examples of humility and patience set by Jesus, Moses, and David. This approach creates a safe space for open dialogue and the possibility of reconciliation.

One way we can support those close to us is by encouraging them to reflect on the many blessings in their own lives and the source of these blessings. Gently helping others to refocus on spiritual priorities can shift their perspective. For example, just as Moses encouraged Joshua not to be jealous but to see the broader picture of God's blessings, we can remind our loved ones of the countless ways God is working in their lives and how their own faithfulness brings glory to Him.

Additionally, we can reflect on how Joseph responded to the jealousy of his brothers. Despite their cruel actions, Joseph maintained his faith in God's plan and later demonstrated forgiveness and kindness when he was in a position of authority. When faced with jealousy from those close to us, we can choose to follow Joseph's example by responding with grace and compassion. Showing humility and a willingness to share credit for achievements can disarm jealousy and foster mutual respect. For instance, we might express gratitude for the support and contributions of others, reinforcing the idea that any success we experience is not just our own, but a reflection of the efforts of those around us.

The story of Jack and John underscores another significant aspect: the danger of trusting advice without examining the advisor's intentions. Psalm 55:21 aptly warns us: "*His words are smoother than butter, but conflict is in his heart. His words are softer than oil, but they are drawn swords.*" John's words, though seemingly helpful, concealed selfish motives. This cautionary tale highlights how envy can lead individuals to manipulate even those they are closest to, eroding trust and sowing discord.

In situations like these, it is vital to approach matters with discernment and prayer. Before acting on advice, seek a second opinion from a trusted confidant, evaluate whether the advice aligns with Biblical principles, and ask for Jehovah's guidance. Open and honest communication can also help clarify intentions and resolve misunderstandings. By maintaining a calm and forgiving demeanor, even when wronged, we can safeguard relationships and promote a spirit of peace. Anchoring ourselves in God's wisdom allows us to navigate such challenges gracefully and avoid falling into the traps of envy or manipulation.

Closing Thoughts

When jealousy arises among those closest to us, it presents an opportunity to imitate Christlike qualities of love, forgiveness, and patience. By focusing on God's wisdom and relying on His guidance, we can transform potentially divisive situations into moments of spiritual growth and unity. This strengthens our relationships with others and deepens our trust in God's ability to work through challenging circumstances for good.

Jesus faced rejection from his own family and community, yet he maintained his focus on doing God's will, never allowing the opinions of others to discourage him. By imitating his example, we can prioritize our relationship with Jehovah, finding reassurance in His love and approval. This mindset enables us to respond to rejection with patience and kindness, paving the way for potential reconciliation.

Additionally, as we reflect on how familiarity can sometimes foster contempt within us, it is important to consider the role of self-examination in overcoming such feelings. When we allow ourselves to critically assess our own hearts, we can uncover the roots of contempt—whether it stems from envy, pride, or a lack of appreciation for the good qualities in others. This kind of introspection is not easy, but it is essential.

In Chapter 11, we will delve deeper into the process of honest self-examination. There, we will explore practical steps to evaluate our thoughts and motives through the lens of

Jehovah's standards. By doing so, we gain the tools to replace bitterness with genuine love and respect, especially toward those we know best.

Chapter 10: God's Correction

H aving explored the destructive roots of jealousy in Chapter 3 and the emotional struggles tied to fairness in Chapter 8, we now delve into the redeeming power of God's correction. This chapter examines how correction, far from being punitive, serves as a guiding force that aligns us with God's standards. Through the examples of Paul and Miriam, we see how humility and responsiveness to discipline pave the way for spiritual growth, unity, and peace.

While it would be unrealistic to assume that most actions influenced by jealousy hinder God's purpose, the biblical examples discussed here offer valuable insights. These accounts demonstrate how such emotions can lead to actions that require external correction and highlight the importance of humility and self-reflection, as well as the necessity of trusting in God's wisdom to address these challenges.

The examples in this chapter showcase God's deep understanding of the human heart and His desire to restore those who are receptive to correction. These accounts reveal how Jehovah, in His wisdom, does not abandon us when we become misguided. Instead, He provides opportunities for us to reflect, adjust our thinking, and grow.

> "My son, do not reject the discipline of Jehovah, and do not loathe his reproof, for those whom Jehovah loves he reproves, just as a father does a son in whom he delights."
> —Proverbs 3:11, 12

God's actions are not merely corrective but deeply instructional, enabling individuals to learn essential lessons about humility, trust, and obedience. By examining these accounts, we can better appreciate the value of correction in refining our qualities and aligning ourselves more closely with God's will. When approached with the right heart condition, this process of correction leads to personal growth and fosters stronger bonds with others.

Through these examples, we are reminded of God's unwavering commitment to our success. He offers discipline, along with the tools needed to thrive under His loving guidance.

The Apostle Paul

One clear example is the apostle Paul (formerly Saul of Tarsus). Before his conversion, Paul was intensely zealous for Judaism and took drastic measures to persecute Christians, viewing them as a threat to his faith. However, his zeal and hostility were redirected through a powerful correction: his encounter with the resurrected Jesus on the road to Damascus.

In Philippians 3:4-6, Paul reflects on his pre-Christian life, describing himself as a "*Hebrew born of Hebrews*" and "*a Pharisee*" who was "*regarding righteousness based on law, one who proved himself blameless.*" His dedication to the Jewish way of life, combined with his rapid rise in influence among his peers, could easily have led him to view the Christians as a threat to his own status and beliefs. In Galatians 1:13-14, Paul emphasizes his zeal and ambition within Judaism, stating, "*I was making greater progress in Judaism than many of my own age in my nation, as I was far more zealous for the traditions of my fathers.*" All of this suggests that his initial opposition to Christians was likely driven more by loyalty to his faith and a sense of duty to protect it. However, it is also entirely possible that he may have harbored some jealousy regarding the increasing influence of Christianity.

Before he embraced the Christian faith, Paul was a zealous Pharisee, highly committed to Jewish traditions and the strict observance of the Mosaic Law. This background may have potentially fueled feelings of jealousy and resentment toward the rapid growth of Christianity, which was drawing many Jews and Gentiles away from traditional Jewish practices and gaining favor among the people.

Acts chapters 7 and 8 provide context for Saul's attitude toward early Christians, particularly around the time of Stephen's martyrdom. In Acts 7:54-58, as Stephen boldly declared his vision of Jesus standing at God's right hand, the enraged Jewish leaders stoned him to death, and Saul was there, approving of the execution. Acts 8:1 states, *"And Saul was taking pleasure with them in his death"* (The Emphasized Bible). This phrase suggests more than casual approval; Saul's strong reaction reflects a deep-seated opposition to the growing Christian movement, possibly fueled by jealousy over the attention, following, and influence that the apostles and early Christians were garnering.

Moreover, Saul's intense persecution of Christians (Acts 8:3) suggests more than mere opposition; it hints at a passionate desire to undermine their work. Acts 9:1-2 describes Saul as *"still breathing threat and murder against the disciples of the Lord"* and securing letters to hunt down Christians in distant cities. This intense reaction appears disproportionate, suggesting an underlying jealousy of the success and attention Christians were gaining, which conflicted with his strong desire to uphold Jewish law and traditions.

Paul's Correction

> *"Saul, Saul, why are you persecuting me?"* —Acts 9:4

In Acts 9:3-6, Jesus confronted Paul, asking why he was persecuting him. This sudden divine intervention opened Paul's eyes—spiritually—to the truth about Jesus and the harm he himself was causing. The encounter led Paul to deeply reassess his actions and attitudes. He humbly accepted correction, was baptized, and redirected his zeal to become one of Christianity's most ardent advocates. Paul's transformation illustrates how Jehovah can use correction to bring about a complete change of heart, offering individuals the opportunity to replace jealousy, hostility, or misguided zeal with qualities that promote unity and love.

Ironically, this very zeal and the persecution of Christians set the stage for Saul's dramatic transformation. His encounter with Jesus on the road to Damascus (Acts 9:3-6) shifted his entire perspective. Rather than being consumed by rivalry, Paul learned to devote his energy to promoting harmony within the Christian congregation and to building up others, even if it meant encouraging those with questionable motives. In

Philippians 1:15-18, he writes, *"True, some are preaching the Christ out of envy and rivalry, but others out of goodwill. With what result? Only that in every way, whether in pretense or in truth, Christ is being proclaimed, and I rejoice over this."* Paul's priority was not his own recognition but the spread of the Christian message. His main focus was on the success of the message, not on who received credit for it. This selfless outlook allowed him to avoid jealousy and to feel genuine joy in seeing the good news reach more people.

Paul's earlier jealousy and opposition were transformed into profound humility and genuine love for all who spread the message, regardless of their background or motivation. Paul consistently encouraged and celebrated the efforts of others, and his attitude provides a potent example of how to rise above jealousy. His journey serves as a powerful testament to how focusing on God's purpose can free us from jealousy, enabling us to rejoice in others' efforts and successes for the sake of the greater good.

Paul often emphasized unity among believers, understanding that division and rivalry could harm the Christian congregation. In 1 Corinthians 3:6-7, he wrote, *"I planted, Apollos watered, but God kept making it grow, so that neither is the one who plants anything nor is the one who waters, but God who makes it grow."* By recognizing that each member played a unique role under God's guidance, Paul encouraged a collaborative spirit, reminding others that all credit belongs to God.

Paul's contentment with his unique calling helped him avoid envy. He described himself as an *"apostle to the nations"* (Romans 11:13), a role he wholeheartedly bore without feeling the need to compete with others. His satisfaction with his own assignment meant he could genuinely encourage others in their ministries without feeling threatened.

Lessons From Paul

The apostle Paul's example offers valuable insights into how to root out jealousy and remain selfless, joyful, and focused on God's purpose. Paul's dramatic experience on the road to

Damascus illustrates how the correction he received refined his thinking and aligned his motives with God's will.

Years later, Paul's transformed state continued to demonstrate his complete acceptance of Jehovah's correction. This lasting transformation enabled him to prioritize the unity of the Christian congregation and the success of the message above personal accolades. Although Paul could have easily felt territorial over his ministry, especially given the many sacrifices he made to spread the good news, his humility in accepting correction allowed him to focus on promoting harmony and cooperation.

Paul's heartfelt words in 1 Thessalonians 2:19-20 capture his joy in seeing others succeed spiritually: *"For what is our hope or joy or crown of exultation before our Lord Jesus at his presence? Is it not in fact you? You certainly are our glory and joy."* These words indicate Paul's selfless focus on the spiritual growth of others rather than on his own achievements. His humility and receptiveness to God's discipline helped him see that valuing the progress of others over personal recognition was essential to maintaining peace.

Another example of God's refining work in Paul's life is evident in his role as an apostle. Paul fully embraced this unique calling, demonstrating no need to compare or compete with others. His joy stemmed from witnessing the spiritual growth of those he served. This appreciation of his role was not innate but rather the result of allowing God's discipline to shape his thinking. The contrast becomes clear when one compares Paul's attitude before his transformation with his outlook afterward.

> *"Keep away from people who try to belittle your ambitions. Small people always do that, but the really great make you feel that you, too, can become great."* —Mark Twain

Mark Twain's observation aligns beautifully with Paul's example. Paul's greatness lay in how he reflected God's qualities, including His love, which "is not jealous" (1 Corinthians 13:4). By applying God's counsel, Paul lifted others up and encouraged them to excel spiritually. This approach strengthened the Christian congregation and brought immense joy to Paul.

As with Paul, God's correction continues to help us today. By accepting His discipline, we can root out any jealousy that may arise and focus on building others up. Just as Paul rejoiced in the success of his spiritual brothers and sisters, we, too, can prioritize the well-being and progress of others. In doing so, we create an environment of mutual encouragement, where we celebrate the growth of those around us and inspire them to reach even greater heights. This selfless mindset allows us to reflect God's love and contribute to the joy of others.

As we reflect on Paul's example, we see how he applied many of the strategies discussed in Chapters 5 and 6 of this book. He worked hard to root out any potential for jealousy within his heart and in the hearts of those around him. By accepting God's correction, Paul achieved success, growth, and contentment. He focused on God's purpose and promoted unity among others, protecting himself from envy and nurturing a spirit of encouragement and joy. In this way, Paul displayed true greatness. He rejoiced in the success of others and helped them excel, reflecting Jehovah's boundless love and wisdom.

Miriam And Aaron

Another powerful example of how God used correction to help individuals overcome envy is found in the story of Moses' siblings. In the previous chapter, we explored how they became jealous of his divinely appointed role by questioning his authority. This situation likely developed over time and stemmed from a combination of personal feelings and circumstances. Miriam, in particular, may have reflected on her earlier role in saving Moses' life as an infant (Exodus 2:4-8) and her later prominence as a prophetess following Israel's deliverance at the Red Sea (Exodus 15:20, 21). These experiences may have caused her to feel entitled to greater recognition and influence.

Aaron played a significant role in the early stages of Israel's deliverance, speaking on Moses' behalf in public settings. Over time, this could have subtly planted seeds of discontent. The siblings may have reasoned that Moses' leadership was not based on any natural ability but solely on God's choice. From their perspective, if Moses needed help to communicate, why was he alone entrusted with such a special and exalted position?

Moses' humility, noted in Numbers 12:3 as *"by far the meekest of all the men on the face of the earth,"* may have further amplified their feelings. His gentle and unassuming nature might have made his leadership appear less imposing, which could have caused Miriam and Aaron to underestimate the seriousness of their challenge to his God-given authority. At the same time, their focus on Moses' perceived weaknesses—compared to their own contributions and abilities—likely fueled their resentment. Miriam, as a prophetess, and Aaron, as Moses' spokesman and later high priest, may have begun to feel overlooked or undervalued.

These thoughts and comparisons eventually led them to question God's arrangement. Their critical words—*"Has he not also spoken through us?"*—indicate a desire for equal prominence and recognition. Pride, comparison, and a longing for validation caused them to lose sight of God's purpose and to fixate on human qualifications. Their flawed perspective blinded them to the reality that God had chosen Moses because of his heart—his humility, loyalty, and faithfulness—not his natural abilities. Ultimately, their jealousy led to God's correction, demonstrating that envy and pride can take root even among those serving in important roles.

Miriam's Correction

Although both Miriam and Aaron felt envious, Miriam appears to have been the primary instigator, as she is mentioned first and was the one directly disciplined by God. The response was swift and direct: God reminded the agitators that Moses held a unique position as His trusted servant, with whom He spoke *"face-to-face."* God clarified His special relationship with Moses, saying, *"I speak to him, openly, not by riddles; and the appearance of Jehovah is what he sees"* (Numbers 12:8), emphasizing Moses' unique role.

To highlight the gravity of their jealousy and disrespect, God struck Miriam with leprosy, which visibly showed His displeasure. Aaron, witnessing this judgment, acknowledged their wrongdoing and immediately pleaded with Moses to intercede for Miriam, saying, "I beg you, my lord! Please do not hold this sin against us! We have acted foolishly in what we have done." (Numbers 12:11). Aaron's plea reflected a recognition of the seriousness of their sin and their desire to restore their relationship with God and with Moses.

Miriam likely reflected on her actions during the seven days she was isolated outside the camp while recovering from her leprosy. This time allowed her to repent and recognize Moses's God-given role. This public act of discipline humbled Miriam and served as a reminder to the entire nation of the dangers of jealousy and the importance of respecting God's arrangements.

God's correction stands in stark contrast to human judgment. While human judgment often stems from partiality or flawed understanding, God's discipline is always motivated by love and is designed to guide us toward growth and restoration. As Hebrews 12:6 states: "For those whom Jehovah loves he disciplines, in fact, he scourges everyone whom he receives as a son." This demonstrates that divine correction is not punitive but an expression of care, aimed at helping us develop qualities that reflect God's perfect standards. By recognizing this distinction, we can welcome correction with humility and gratitude, knowing it is a sign of His deep concern for our well-being.

After her discipline and restoration, there is no further record of Miriam or Aaron displaying jealousy toward Moses. Miriam's repentance, coupled with God's discipline, effectively transformed her attitude. She resumed her supportive role in the nation, alongside her brothers, indicating that she had accepted God's arrangement and let go of her jealous feelings.

Lessons From Miriam And Aaron

"Obedience is the mother of success and is wedded to safety." —Aeschylus

Aeschylus was an ancient Greek playwright, and his works often focused on the tension between human hubris and divine will. His quote underscores the wisdom of respecting established arrangements. It reminds us that success and security come not from seeking prominence or disregarding divine order, but from humbly obeying those in authority. The story of Miriam and Aaron provides a vivid illustration of this principle. By challenging God's arrangement, they created division, jeopardized their relationship with Moses, and risked their standing before Jehovah. God's response illustrated that obedience to His arrangement is essential for unity and spiritual safety. Once Miriam and Aaron accepted their error, peace was restored.

God's correction in this account highlights His love and fairness. When He corrected Miriam, He aimed to emphasize the gravity of her misconduct and the necessity for sincere repentance. The time Miriam spent in isolation allowed her time to reflect on her feelings and actions, reinforcing the idea that discipline is often necessary to help us recognize and overcome wrong motives. Hebrews 12:11 reminds us that "No discipline seems for the present to be joyous, but it is painful; yet afterward, it yields the peaceable fruit of righteousness to those who have been trained by it." Miriam's story confirms that God's correction, though challenging, is an expression of His love, designed to guide us back to a place of harmony with Him and others.

Miriam's journey highlights how correction can lead to self-reflection and repentance, ultimately restoring peace. By humbly accepting God's correction, she was able to renew her heart, let go of envy, and return to her supportive role alongside Moses and Aaron. This teaches us that, no matter how difficult it may seem to change our emotions or attitudes, God's guidance and correction can help us achieve it. The story of Miriam and Aaron encourages us to approach feelings of jealousy honestly, seek God's direction, and trust that, with His help, we can cultivate peace, respect, and unity in our relationships.

Correction That Leads To Growth And Unity

The examples of the apostle Paul and Miriam beautifully illustrate Jehovah's loving and purposeful use of correction to address jealousy and misguided attitudes. Far from being harsh, God's discipline serves as an opportunity for self-reflection, transformation, and growth. Paul's dramatic encounter on the road to Damascus and Miriam's period of isolation both highlight God's desire to help individuals realign their thinking.

When we humbly accept God's correction, we experience profound benefits. Paul's transformation freed him from rivalry, enabling him to find joy in the success of others. Similarly, Miriam's restoration allowed her to overcome envy and resume her role in harmony with God's arrangement.

Today, we can draw encouragement from these lessons. When feelings of jealousy or rivalry arise, reflecting on God's wisdom can help us cultivate humility and joy in the successes of others. Just as Paul and Miriam grew through correction, we, too, can allow God's loving guidance to refine us. By accepting His discipline and trusting in His arrangement, we strengthen our relationship with Him and contribute to unity and peace. In this way, Jehovah's correction becomes a blessing—one that brings us closer to Him and to one another.

Correction often comes through three primary means: God's Word, our conscience, and loving counsel from others. Understanding these sources helps us align our responses to God's guidance and grow spiritually.

Prayerful Introspection

When correction comes, taking time to reflect and pray can help us identify where adjustments are needed. Psalm 139:23, 24 encourages us to pray:

> "Search through me, O God, and know my heart. Examine me, and know my anxious thoughts. See whether there is in me any harmful way, and lead me in the way of eternity."
> —Psalm 139:23, 24

This heartfelt request invites God to guide our thinking and refine our character, allowing us to respond to discipline with gratitude rather than resistance. As discussed in Chapter 6, self-examination is essential for cultivating humility and avoiding jealousy. Prayerfully inviting Jehovah to examine our motives strengthens our ability to recognize correction as an opportunity for growth.

Seeking Guidance From God's Word

The Bible is a powerful tool for identifying areas in need of improvement. The first portion of Hebrews 4:12 reminds us:

> "For the word of God is alive and exerts power and is sharper than any two-edged sword and pierces even to the dividing of soul and spirit." —Hebrews 4:12

By studying specific scriptures that address our challenges, we can better align our actions with God's standards. Cain's failure to heed God's direct guidance highlights the consequences of ignoring divine counsel. Chapter 7 emphasizes the importance of seeking guidance proactively to avoid falling into the destructive patterns of jealousy and resentment.

Accepting Counsel From Others

Sometimes, Jehovah provides correction through trusted friends or family. Proverbs 27:6 states:

> "The wounds inflicted by a friend are faithful." —Proverbs 27:6

While counsel may feel uncomfortable, it reflects a genuine desire to help us improve. Viewing such guidance as an expression of love enables us to embrace it with a positive spirit. The principles of humility and collaboration from

Chapter 5 equip us to accept counsel graciously, recognizing it as a tool for cultivating unity and spiritual growth.

Applying The Lessons

Correction is valuable only when acted upon. James 1:22 advises, "*Become doers of the word and not hearers only, deceiving yourselves with false reasoning.*" Studying God's Word, prayerfully examining ourselves, and lovingly responding to discipline demonstrate our commitment to spiritual growth. Reflecting on how discipline can shape our character aligns with the themes of introspection and gratitude explored in Chapter 11.

Jehovah's correction refines us, enabling us to cultivate a heart of humility, gratitude, and love. This approach ensures that discipline becomes a stepping stone toward peace and righteousness.

Chapter 11: Reflection

Beyond the power of God's correction discussed in the previous chapter, the Bible emphasizes the transformative role of reflection in overcoming negative attitudes. In Chapter 6, we explored how self-reflection can uncover hidden struggles. However, the significant impact of self-reflection in uprooting jealousy and enhancing our well-being warrants further exploration. In this chapter, we will delve deeper into the life-changing effects of this practice when guided by God's wisdom.

When we recognize harmful behaviors within us, take the time to reflect on them, and take deliberate steps to correct them, we can often avoid harsher discipline from God later. This process requires humility, self-awareness, and a genuine desire to align our actions with God's will.

Jealousy can consume us, shattering our tranquility and gradually diminishing our happiness. Therefore, as an act of kindness toward ourselves, we need to take immediate action to restore that balance and happiness—especially since the power to change lies within our own hands. Every moment we delay only prolongs the harm we endure. By proactively examining and adjusting our motives, we can free ourselves from the emotional toll of jealousy and move toward a more fulfilling and harmonious life.

Although the Bible contains fewer explicit accounts of individuals proactively addressing jealousy, its principles clarify that those who sincerely examine their hearts and align their thoughts with Jehovah's standards can overcome destructive emotions and behaviors. These examples remind us that internal change, while often challenging, is both achievable and deeply rewarding. It can lead to healing, restored relationships, and significant spiritual growth. By allowing God's Word and principles to shape our hearts and guide our actions, we invite His wisdom and love to transform us from within.

Asaph's Struggle

> "For I became envious of the arrogant when I would see the peace of the wicked" —Psalm 73:3

Asaph, a psalmist, offers a deeply personal and instructive account of overcoming envy through introspection. In Psalm 73:3, he openly acknowledges his internal conflict. Witnessing the apparent prosperity of those who disregarded God, Asaph felt disheartened, questioning why the righteous often endure hardships while the wicked appear to thrive. This honest reflection resonates with a universal human challenge: reconciling life's injustices with faith in divine justice.

Asaph's turmoil persisted until he sought God's perspective. In Psalm 73:16-17, he writes, "When I tried to understand it, it was troubling to me. Until I entered the grand sanctuary of God, and I discerned their future." By meditating on God's justice and purpose, Asaph came to realize that the success of the wicked is temporary, fleeting like a dream. This spiritual clarity allowed him to understand their ultimate end—God's judgment —and to refocus on the enduring blessings that come from loyalty to Jehovah. Asaph concluded that drawing close to God was far more valuable than any fleeting advantages the wicked might enjoy.

Life often provides clarity in hindsight. Looking back, we can see how certain experiences have shaped us. But what if we could gain such understanding before making decisions or forming opinions? This is what Asaph achieved by seeking God's perspective. Rather than being swept away by appearances, he reasoned from a spiritual viewpoint, discerning the likely outcomes of the wicked's actions and aligning his thoughts with divine wisdom.

Today, like Asaph, when faced with challenges that seem unfair, we can pause to consider the bigger picture. For instance, imagine seeing classmates cheating on an exam and scoring higher grades. At first, it may seem that integrity offers no reward. However, reasoning through the consequences reveals that dishonesty often leads to negative outcomes, whereas honesty fosters a clean conscience and God's approval—blessings that outweigh temporary gains.

Proverbs 22:3 reminds us, "*The shrewd one sees the danger and conceals himself, but the inexperienced keep right on going and suffer the consequences.*" Relying on God's wisdom, as revealed in His Word, equips us to anticipate outcomes and avoid unnecessary pitfalls. Reflecting on scriptures about the consequences of greed, immorality, or materialism helps us steer clear of choices that may seem appealing but ultimately bring sorrow.

Asaph concluded in Psalm 73:28, "*But as for me, drawing near to God is good for me.*" Developing closeness to Jehovah gives us the foresight and strength to navigate life's challenges with peace and confidence, knowing His justice is perfect. By trusting Him, we secure blessings that endure—not just in hindsight but in the present and into the future.

Asaph's experience underscores how easy it is to fall into envy when comparing ourselves to others. His turning point came when he entered God's sanctuary and gained clarity. In worship, he saw the transience of worldly success and refocused on God's enduring blessings.

Asaph's reflections mirror the gratitude expressed by the Sons of Korah in their psalms. Both teach us that true happiness is found not in envying others but in drawing close to God, as they sang, "*For a day in your courtyards is better than a thousand anywhere else!*" (Psalm 84:10) Worship helps us reframe our focus and find joy in spiritual blessings.

The Value Of Introspection

Asaph's willingness to confront his feelings and meditate on God's justice highlights the importance of introspection. Rather than suppressing or ignoring his jealousy, Asaph courageously examined his emotions. This required honesty and humility—traits necessary for realigning his perspective with God's standards.

Self-reflection can be uncomfortable, as it forces us to confront the ugly parts of ourselves that we might prefer to keep hidden. For Asaph, recognizing that his envy stemmed from focusing too much on the temporary prosperity of the wicked must have been humbling. Initially, he might have justified his feelings by fixating on perceived injustices, but he ultimately acknowledged that the problem was in his incorrect perspective, not in God's justice. This moment of clarity became the turning point that corrected his flawed thinking. Asaph shifted his focus from temporal appearances to eternal truths, which resolved his inner turmoil and strengthened both his faith and contentment.

Asaph's example shows that self-examination, though challenging, is vital for overcoming jealousy. Admitting we are wrong requires humility, but it is the first step toward aligning our thoughts with God's standards. Proverbs 3:5-6 advises, *"Trust in Jehovah with all your heart, and do not rely on your own understanding. In all your ways take notice of him, and he will make your paths straight."* When we approach God with an open heart, ready to adjust our thinking, we benefit from His wisdom.

Rather than fearing introspection, we can embrace it as an opportunity for growth. Honest self-reflection allows us to uncover areas where we can draw closer to God and see the temporary nature of life's challenges more clearly. Like Asaph, by confronting and addressing our emotions, we move toward a deeper trust in God's love and justice, and we build stronger, more peaceful relationships.

Finding Peace Through Prayer

After examining his emotions and recognizing the need for change, Asaph turned to God in prayer. Prayer is a crucial step in overcoming jealousy and other negative emotions. It allows us to express our concerns and helps us gain God's perspective and find the strength to adjust our thinking. Through heartfelt prayer, Asaph demonstrated trust in God's ability to provide clarity.

Turning to God in prayer offers a safe space to process overwhelming emotions. Psalm 65:2 refers to Jehovah as the "Hearer of prayer," emphasizing His willingness to listen and provide guidance. Like Asaph, when we approach God with honesty and humility, we open ourselves to His solutions, which shift our focus to divine priorities.

Philippians 4:6-7 assures us that peace comes when we trust God to help us navigate life's challenges and realign our thinking with His wisdom. It states:

> "Do not be anxious over anything, but in everything by prayer and supplication along with thanksgiving, let your petitions be made known to God; and the peace of God that surpasses all understanding will guard your hearts and your mental powers." —Philippians 4:6-7

Prayer strengthens our relationship with God, empowering us to overcome negative feelings. By regularly seeking His guidance, we find comfort and assurance in His love and justice, which far outweigh temporary inequities or struggles.

Joseph's Brothers

There are many lessons to be learned from the account of Joseph in the Bible, both from the good example set by him and from the actions of his brothers. Like Asaph, Joseph's brothers faced internal conflicts, and Jehovah did not give them direct correction or a warning at the time of their jealous actions. Still, their later expressions of guilt and remorse indicate that they eventually recognized the severity of their wrongdoing. Their journey reveals how, even in the absence of immediate divine intervention or counsel, a well-trained conscience can guide individuals toward powerful self-reflection and eventual change.

Years after they sold Joseph into slavery, famine forced his brothers to travel to Egypt in search of food, where they unknowingly encountered their brother, who was now a high-ranking official. When Joseph tested them by accusing them of being spies and imprisoning them, they showed remorse and confessed to each other by saying:

> "We are surely being punished on account of our brother, because we saw his distress when he begged us to show compassion, but we did not listen." —Genesis 42:21

One might argue that the famine and the pressures Joseph placed on his brothers acted as catalysts, essentially compelling them to reflect and change, potentially diminishing the value of entirely unprompted self-reflection. However, their account still highlights the transformative power of reflection, showing that true change often requires a genuine internal willingness to confront and address past wrongs.

God's design of the human conscience is an expression of His wisdom and love. A well-trained conscience, informed by Jehovah's moral standards, serves as an internal guide, steering individuals back toward righteousness. In Joseph's brothers' case, their consciences preserved a clear memory of their cruelty and reminded them of God's justice, encouraged self-examination, and ultimately helped prepare them for reconciliation. When Joseph tested their sincerity by challenging their honesty and loyalty, they responded in ways that showed their consciences had been actively influencing their hearts.

Their remorse intensified as they found themselves in distress in Egypt, much like the distress they had caused Joseph. This "reaping what they sowed" helped them empathize with his suffering and allowed them to reflect more deeply on the gravity of their jealousy. Later, when Joseph demanded that they bring Benjamin back to Egypt, Judah offered to stay in his younger brother's place, demonstrating a willingness to sacrifice himself for the well-being of his family (Genesis 44:33). This shift in attitude suggests that they had learned a profound lesson from their past, showing a transformation of heart and a newfound humility.

When we face the consequences of our actions, we gain valuable insight into how our behavior affects both ourselves and others. Jehovah often uses these moments as opportunities to teach us, helping us understand why attitudes like jealousy or selfishness are harmful. By reflecting on these experiences with an open heart, we can foster genuine repentance, learn humility, and develop greater empathy for those around us. This is exactly what Judah and the rest of Joseph's brothers came to understand through their experience. Such moments of self-reflection become opportunities for growth, enabling us to cultivate a spirit of compassion, move beyond our past mistakes, and, where possible, make amends.

The Power Of A Well-Trained Conscience

Although the Bible does not provide details about what happened in Joseph's paternal home during the more than 20 years he was in Egypt, this silence does not mean that nothing significant occurred. The absence of evidence is not evidence of absence; meaningful developments can and often do happen, even without being explicitly mentioned. Joseph's brothers were raised in a household where God's standards were taught and valued, and this upbringing likely shaped their moral compass. Despite their earlier failure to listen to their consciences in the heat of jealousy, their later expressions of regret suggest that these lessons remained with them. Over time, the well-trained conscience that Jehovah instilled in them began to guide their thoughts, eventually helping them recognize and acknowledge their wrongdoing.

This experience underscores the value of training our conscience according to God's standards. Just as Joseph's brothers were eventually led to repentance and reconciliation, we too can benefit from consistently aligning our moral compass with God's Word. By doing so, our conscience can serve as a powerful guide to help us make changes, repair relationships, and remain on the path of righteousness.

Thus, while God did not give Joseph's brothers an immediate warning, their well-trained consciences and repentance show that God often allows time and circumstances to guide people toward self-awareness. The brothers' journey of introspection and regret serves as a reminder that unresolved jealousy has a way of resurfacing, pushing us to confront the pain we may have caused others. Our conscience, therefore, acts as an inner moral compass that helps us distinguish right from wrong. When we ignore this gift, we risk allowing harmful emotions to grow.

Our conscience functions as a retrospective guide and an early warning system, alerting us to attitudes and actions that may displease God. In moments of self-reflection, our conscience can remind us of the importance of aligning our actions with

His standards. Romans 2:13-14 highlights how Jehovah has given everyone a conscience. These verses illustrate how it serves as a guiding light, revealing our intentions and helping us examine our motives. Listening to our conscience helps us maintain a good relationship with God, which brings us peace and a sense of closeness to Him.

Continue Training Your Conscience

> *"Labor to keep alive in your breast that little spark of celestial fire called conscience."* —George Washington

Washington reminds us that our conscience is a precious, divinely inspired guide that requires effort and attentiveness to keep alive. Maintaining a strong, active conscience does not happen passively; it requires deliberate effort to remain sensitive to God's standards and open to His guidance. We need to develop a good conscience by regularly reflecting on our actions, reasons, and attitudes, just as we tend to a small flame to keep it from going out. This "spark" of conscience helps us distinguish right from wrong, urging us toward honesty, integrity, and compassion. By keeping this inner guide active, we allow it to shape our choices and encourage positive change even when faced with difficult decisions.

Ignoring our conscience, however, can lead us down a dangerous path, allowing negative traits to take root. When we disregard these internal warnings, we risk becoming calloused, justifying actions that go against God's standards, and damaging our relationships with others. The conscience, when heeded, serves as a protective guide that leads us back to Jehovah's ways, but when ignored, it can lose its sensitivity, making it harder for us to feel remorse or seek change. By valuing and responding to our conscience, we remain spiritually sensitive, allowing God to mold our character and lead us toward qualities like empathy, humility, and love that strengthen our bond with others.

The Value Of Reflection

The account of Asaph and the journey of Joseph's brothers both accentuate the transformative power of internal reflection, especially when paired with prayer and reliance on God. These examples demonstrate that even deeply ingrained emotions, such as envy and bitterness, can be addressed and overcome through honest self-examination and a willingness to align one's thoughts with God's guidance. Whether facing feelings of envy, as Asaph did; or the guilt and remorse that weighed on Joseph's brothers, internal reflection emerges as a crucial step in restoring peace and spiritual clarity.

Recognizing The Need For Change

Asaph's willingness to confront his feelings and acknowledge his flawed perspective led him to seek God's guidance. Similarly, the Sons of Korah, in Psalm 49, reflect on the fleeting nature of wealth and the futility of material pursuits. This meditation can help us reframe our perspective and rise above jealousy, focusing on eternal blessings rather than temporary gains.

Joseph's brothers offer another perspective on the power of internal reflection, particularly in the absence of immediate divine intervention. After selling Joseph into slavery, they apparently ignored their conscience for years; however, their guilt and remorse eventually surfaced when they faced distressing circumstances in Egypt. Their change of heart, spurred by reflection, led them to reexamine their motives and ultimately demonstrate a transformed spirit of humility and empathy.

Relying On God's Guidance

Internal reflection is not merely about identifying areas for improvement; it also involves recognizing God's role in helping us change. Psalm 37:5 encourages: "*Commit your way to Jehovah; rely on Him, and He will act in your behalf.*" By leaning on God, we find the strength to reshape our thinking, enabling us to overcome negative emotions that could otherwise dominate our hearts.

Asaph and Joseph's brothers each relied on God in their own ways to reshape their thinking and correct their attitudes. For Asaph, entering "the grand sanctuary of God" (Psalm 73:17) brought clarity about the fleeting nature of the wicked's prosperity and helped him refocus on God's enduring justice. For Joseph's brothers, a well-trained conscience, shaped by their upbringing according to God's standards, helped guide them toward repentance and reconciliation. In these cases, God's guidance proved essential in transforming harmful emotions.

A Path To Peace And Spiritual Growth

Internal reflection, guided by prayer and meditation on God's thoughts, leads to growth, peace, and a closer relationship with Him. This transformative process helps us navigate life's challenges with humility and clarity, aligning our hearts with God's purpose. By reflecting on His Word and allowing His principles to shape our motives and actions, we safeguard our relationships and experience lasting contentment. As Proverbs 20:27 reminds us:

> "The breath of a man is the lamp of Jehovah, searching through his innermost being." —Proverbs 20:27

This divine "lamp" of conscience, when nurtured through regular self-examination, serves as a guiding light, helping us discern right from wrong. By embracing internal reflection, we invite Jehovah to mold us, assist us in overcoming harmful emotions, and cultivate a heart filled with happiness and peace.

Chapter 12: Can Jealousy Be Avoided?

J ealousy is such an innate and deeply rooted human emotion that it often seems unavoidable. This raises important questions: Can jealousy truly be avoided, or is it an inherent challenge of human imperfection? Is it truly possible to live without experiencing jealousy, or is it something we must learn to recognize and manage instead of completely evading?

The Bible contains inspiring examples of individuals who demonstrated a remarkable ability to rise above jealousy, even in situations where envy might have seemed natural or justified. For example, Jonathan's loyalty to David, highlighted in Chapters 5 and 7, exemplifies how love and respect for God's arrangement can conquer jealousy, fostering lasting relationships. He resisted the temptation to let jealousy take root and displayed qualities that allowed him to remain steadfast in his love for Jehovah and in his relationships with others.

While some may appear to have a natural disposition toward humility and selflessness, their actions reveal a deliberate choice to cultivate key traits that empower them to reject jealousy. This chapter will consider biblical characters who displayed remarkable faith, love, humility, respect, and contentment—all traits worthy of closer examination and development in our lives. By understanding and imitating these traits, we too can learn to avoid jealousy and foster a spirit of love and unity.

John The Baptist

John the Baptist was a prominent preacher, drawing large crowds and gathering a substantial following as he prepared people for the coming of the Messiah. However, when Jesus' ministry began to grow, and more people started following him, John had every reason to feel protective or even envious. However, John's response reflected his humility, satisfaction, and clarity about his purpose within God's plan.

John understood that his purpose was to prepare the way for the Messiah. His role was divinely appointed, and he saw himself as a servant in God's arrangement, tasked with setting the stage for Jesus. In John 1:23, he quoted Isaiah, saying, "*I am a voice of someone crying out in the wilderness, 'Make the way of Jehovah straight.*'" By embracing this purpose, John felt no need to compete with Jesus. He viewed Jesus' success as a fulfillment of his own mission, rather than as a threat to it.

When some of John's disciples expressed concern that Jesus was attracting more followers, John responded with humility and acceptance, saying, "*A man cannot receive a single thing unless it has been given to him from heaven*" (John 3:27). John understood that any position or distinction he possessed was bestowed upon him by God. He was willing to step back to facilitate the growth of Jesus' ministry, valuing God's purpose above his own status.

Lessons From John The Baptist

John found joy in fulfilling his assignment rather than in the attention he received. His primary focus was on helping others recognize the Messiah. By directing people to Jesus and encouraging them to follow him, John demonstrated a selfless love for God's purpose. This joy in service, rather than in personal success, protected him from jealousy and allowed him to celebrate Jesus' growth with genuine happiness.

John's spiritual maturity enabled him to avoid feelings of rivalry. He was aware of the temporary nature of his role, and rather than clinging to his own popularity, he accepted that his purpose was to pass the baton to Jesus. In John 3:29, he described himself as "*the friend of the bridegroom,*" finding joy in hearing the bridegroom's voice. This metaphor highlights John's profound self-awareness and his satisfaction with being a supporter rather than the central figure, enabling him to rise above any feelings of competition.

John the Baptist's example teaches us the importance of humility, self-awareness, and maintaining a clear focus on God's purpose. Despite being a prominent preacher, John never viewed Jesus's growing popularity as a threat. He had a strong sense of purpose, understanding that his role was to prepare the way for the Messiah. Rather than seeking to be the main figure, he prioritized God's arrangement over personal recognition.

John found genuine joy in serving God's will rather than seeking attention or validation. By directing others to Jesus, he demonstrated selfless love, which protected him from jealousy. His emotional awareness enabled him to embrace his temporary role and rejoice in the fulfillment of God's purpose.

John's example inspires us to embrace our individual contributions and to genuinely applaud the achievements of others without experiencing any sense of inadequacy. Ultimately, his life shows that when we remain focused on a higher purpose and are content with our place in God's plan, we can avoid rivalry and experience true fulfillment.

Moses

Moses, one of the most prominent figures in biblical history, was chosen by Jehovah to lead the Israelites out of Egypt and through the wilderness. Despite facing numerous challenges and opposition, Moses exemplified remarkable humility and faith throughout his leadership. His meekness, coupled with his unwavering trust in God, enabled him to navigate potential conflicts and avoid falling into the trap of jealousy, even when his authority was questioned. His reaction to circumstances that could have provoked envy offers important lessons on maintaining a humble and selfless attitude in positions of responsibility.

Throughout his life, Moses demonstrated an extraordinary ability to navigate leadership challenges with humility and love. In Chapters 9 and 10, we explored how Moses handled the jealousy of his siblings, Miriam and Aaron, with remarkable grace. He chose to intercede on Miriam's behalf when God disciplined her, prioritizing unity over retaliation. This account underscores Moses' unwavering reliance on God and his deep concern for the spiritual welfare of others.

This chapter will focus on yet another event that showcases Moses' humility and dedication to God's will—the account of Eldad and Medad. This episode reveals Moses' exceptional ability to rise above personal pride and rejoice in the empowerment of others, demonstrating a love for God's arrangement and the people he served.

Appointed by God to lead Israel, Moses had every reason to protect his unique role. Yet when two men, Eldad and Medad, began prophesying in the camp, Moses displayed humility rather than jealousy. His response to this situation shows important ways to deal with feelings of rivalry.

Moses understood that his position as leader was not self-appointed but given by God. This divine appointment made him confident in his role, freeing him from the need to defend his authority. When Joshua suggested stopping Eldad and Medad, Moses replied, "Are you jealous for me? No, I wish that all of Jehovah's people were prophets and that Jehovah would put his spirit on them!" (Numbers 11:29). His words show that he didn't see others' spiritual gifts as a threat to his position, but rather as a blessing for the entire nation.

Moses' humility is a recurring theme in his life. Numbers 12:3 describes him as "by far the meekest of all the men on the face of the earth." Rather than elevating his own position, Moses viewed himself as a servant to the people and to God. His meekness allowed him to see Eldad and Medad's prophesying not as competition, but as a sign of God's active presence among the people.

Moses recognized that the work was not about himself but about fulfilling God's will. By focusing on the bigger picture of leading Israel toward the Promised Land, he avoided being sidetracked by feelings of rivalry. He understood that the success of his mission was more important than his personal status. This focus helped him avoid the trap of jealousy and instead foster a spirit of unity and encouragement.

Lessons From Moses

Moses' life demonstrates that true leadership involves prioritizing the spiritual growth and welfare of others; it involves uplifting others, not holding them back. His ability to rejoice in the success of others, even when it could have been seen as a challenge to his position, shows a strong example of staying humble.

He sincerely desired that all of God's people could share in spiritual blessings. His unselfish outlook allowed him to welcome others' success and giftedness without feeling diminished. His desire for others to experience God's spirit showed a love for the people that superseded personal pride or rivalry.

By focusing on God's will rather than personal ambition, Moses avoided feelings of rivalry. This mindset serves as a reminder to prioritize collective goals over personal recognition. His meekness allowed him to remain calm and focused when challenged. His example shows that meekness is not a weakness but a quality that fosters unity and trust.

By reflecting on Moses' example, we can learn to approach our responsibilities with humility, support the growth of others, and maintain our focus on fulfilling Jehovah's purpose.

Hannah

Among all the outstanding women of faith in the Bible, Hannah arguably faced some of the strongest temptations to feel jealous. Yet, her resolve to resist jealousy's pull makes her an extraordinary example of how to overcome it entirely. Her life provides a powerful lesson in trusting God and finding emotional relief through prayer, resilience, and reliance on Him.

While Chapter 8 explores how she trusted in God's fairness amidst emotional challenges, this chapter focuses on her resilient spirit and gratitude after receiving God's blessings. When Jehovah answered her fervent prayers by granting her a son, Hannah did not cling possessively to her child. Instead, she fulfilled her vow by dedicating Samuel to God's service (1 Samuel 1:27-28).

Hannah's trial was harrowing—she was childless in a society where bearing children was highly esteemed. To make matters worse, her rival wife, Peninnah, who had children, taunted and provoked her unceasingly. The Bible vividly describes how Peninnah *"taunted her relentlessly to upset her"* because of her childlessness, causing Hannah significant distress (1 Samuel 1:6, 7). Each year, as the family went up to the house of God, Peninnah's provocations intensified, compounding Hannah's grief and reminding her of what she lacked. This prolonged hardship was not a fleeting challenge but an ongoing trial that tested Hannah's emotional and spiritual resilience year after year.

What made Hannah's response remarkable was her decision not to let Peninnah's provocations define her character. Despite her pain and sadness about not being able to have children, she refused to let jealousy take root in her heart. Instead, Hannah turned to God in heartfelt prayer. She poured out her anguish, openly expressing her deepest feelings to Him and placing her trust in His ability to provide relief.

Hannah's heartfelt vow in 1 Samuel 1:11 reveals the depth of her faith and selflessness. When she prayed to God for a child, she promised, *"If you look upon the affliction of your servant and remember me and you do not forget your servant and give to your servant a male child, I will give him to Jehovah all the days of his life."* This prayer was not driven by selfish ambition or pride but by a sincere desire to honor God. Her longing for a child went beyond fulfilling personal emotional needs; she desired to dedicate him to God's service. This reflects her remarkable spiritual maturity and her willingness to prioritize God's will over her own feelings.

In time, God blessed Hannah by answering her prayer—a reminder that trusting in His timing and justice can bring great rewards.

Lessons From Hannah

Hannah's actions echo other extraordinary examples of faith in the Bible. Like Abraham, who was willing to offer Isaac in obedience to God's command (Genesis 22:9-12), Hannah demonstrated absolute trust in God by being ready to give up what she desired most. Both accounts underscore that blessings come from prioritizing God's will above personal desires. Abraham's faith was rewarded when God spared Isaac, and Hannah's heartfelt prayer was answered with the birth of Samuel.

These examples show that when we give up something important for God, He rewards us with something even better. Abraham received his son back along with the assurance of God's blessings upon his descendants. Similarly, Hannah's selfless dedication of Samuel brought her peace, fulfillment, and the privilege of being the mother of a pivotal servant in God's purpose—Samuel, a faithful prophet and judge in Israel.

This aligns with Proverbs 3:9-10: "*Honor Jehovah with your valuable things, with the firstfruits of all your produce; Then your storehouses will be completely filled, and your vats will overflow with new wine.*" By giving our best to God, we demonstrate trust in Him and open the way for abundant blessings. The experiences of Hannah and Abraham affirm this principle, encouraging us to prioritize God's will and trust His promises.

Additionally, these examples foreshadow God's willingness to give His most treasured possession—His Son, Jesus Christ—as a sacrifice for humankind (John 3:16). Just as Abraham and Hannah entrusted their sons to God's care, God entrusted His Son to carry out the greatest act of love, providing salvation for those who exercise faith. Such acts of trust and selflessness highlight the importance of prioritizing the needs of others over our own (Matthew 6:33).

Hannah's story inspires us to examine our motivations in prayer and service. Are we seeking blessings for personal gain, or are we motivated by a desire to glorify God and support His purpose? Her selflessness in dedicating Samuel glorified God and safeguarded her against jealousy. By focusing on God's will, she turned her pain into gain. This perspective allowed her to replace any potential feelings of bitterness with peace and joy.

Like Hannah, we can strive to make God's will our priority. Trusting that He will provide for us in ways that exceed our expectations demonstrates a type of faith and devotion that mirrors the selflessness of Hannah, Abraham, and God Himself.

> "'Bring the entire tithe into the storehouse, so that there may be food in my house; and test me out, please, in this regard,' Jehovah of armies says, 'to see whether I will not open to you the floodgates of the heavens and pour out on you a blessing until there is nothing lacking.'" —Malachi 3:10

Insights From John, Moses, And Hannah

The accounts of John the Baptist, Moses, and Hannah reveal key attitudes that help guard against jealousy. Each of these faithful servants faced situations that could have triggered rivalry; yet, they chose to focus on God's will, setting aside personal ambition for the greater good. Hannah, in particular, demonstrated remarkable selflessness by dedicating her son Samuel to God's service, even though she had long yearned for a child. Her willingness to place God's purpose above her own desires reflects a heart free from jealousy.

Together, John, Moses, and Hannah exemplify that genuine fulfillment stems from a defined purpose, modesty, and a sincere commitment to uplifting others. They encourage us to trust in God's arrangement, find joy in seeing others succeed, and maintain a selfless attitude that unifies and uplifts.

Their examples provide unique insights into how embracing key characteristics in cultivating godly qualities can help us avoid jealousy. Their actions reveal that resisting jealousy is not an automatic response but rather the result of deliberate effort, guided by faith and reliance on Jehovah. These individuals demonstrated that maintaining focus on God's will and embracing selfless attitudes can free the heart from rivalry and envy. Through their examples, we can identify five key character traits that enable us to rise above jealousy: faith, love, humility, respect, and contentment.

1. Strong Faith

John demonstrated strong faith in God's arrangement and did not feel threatened or envious. He acknowledged that we received all things from above (John 3:27). His faith helped him focus on fulfilling his purpose of preparing the way for the Messiah, trusting in God's greater plan and rejoicing in Jesus' success. This is reflected in his words in John 1:29, where he said concerning Jesus: "*See, the Lamb of God who takes away the sin of the world!*"

Moses also exhibited remarkable faith throughout his life, trusting in God even when faced with difficult circumstances. When challenged by Korah, Dathan, and Abiram, who questioned his leadership and sought to elevate themselves, Moses did not react defensively or assert his authority out of pride. Instead, he placed the matter in God's hands, saying, "*In the morning Jehovah will make known who belongs to Him and who is holy.*" (Numbers 16:5). Moses' faith in God's justice allowed him to remain calm and humble, confident that God would vindicate him. This trust in God's arrangement, even in the face of rebellion, demonstrates the depth of Moses' faith and his focus on God's will.

Despite enduring years of ridicule and disappointment, Hannah's faith was evident in her fervent prayers to God. She did not allow her sorrow to drive her away from God but turned to Him with heartfelt sincerity. Her prayer in 1 Samuel 1:11, in which she vowed to dedicate her child to God if He would grant her a son, reflects her deep trust in His power and justice. By placing her hope entirely in God, Hannah demonstrated a faith that transcended her circumstances.

2. Genuine Love

John demonstrated genuine love by prioritizing the spiritual growth of others. When his followers struggled with Jesus' increasing influence, John redirected their focus to God's will, encouraging them to follow Jesus as the Messiah.

On another occasion, John's love for people shone through in his practical and compassionate guidance, aimed at helping them live in harmony with God's standards. When crowds asked him what they should do, John responded with counsel that reflected deep care for their spiritual and social well-being. He encouraged them, saying, "Let the man who has two garments share with the man who has none, and let the one who has something to eat do the same." (Luke 3:11). This advice demonstrated John's concern for fostering love and unity among the people, urging them to reflect God's qualities of kindness and compassion in their daily interactions. His message was not just about repentance; it was about helping people embody the love that comes from serving Jehovah.

In Chapter 10, we examined the account of how, instead of seeking vindication, Moses immediately prayed for Miriam's healing when she and Aaron spoke against him out of jealousy (Numbers 12:13). His quickness to forgive and to seek God's mercy for his sister underscores his love for others.

On another occasion, Moses pleaded with God to forgive the Israelites when they sinned by worshiping the golden calf, even offering to have his own name blotted out from God's book in their place (Exodus 32:32). His willingness to sacrifice his standing with God for the sake of the people demonstrated profound love and compassion for their spiritual recovery.

Hannah's deep love for God is vividly displayed in her reaction to God's blessing. Instead of keeping her long-awaited son for herself, she demonstrated her devotion by fulfilling her vow and dedicating Samuel to God's service, as seen in 1 Samuel 1:24-28. This act of selflessness reflected her heartfelt desire to honor God above her own desires. Her prayer of thanksgiving in 1 Samuel 2:1-10 further reveals her deep love and reverence for God, as she praised His unmatched righteousness and celebrated His care for the humble and faithful. Her actions demonstrate that genuine love and trust in God's will can overcome even the deepest emotional pain.

3. Humility

John the Baptist's humility was evident in his acknowledgment of Jesus' superior role in God's arrangement. He stated in John 1:27 that he was not worthy even to untie the straps of Jesus' sandals, a task regarded as the lowest duty of a servant. This vivid expression stressed John's deep understanding of his role as a forerunner to the Messiah. Despite his growing influence, John consistently directed attention away from himself, emphasizing that his mission was solely to prepare the way for someone far greater. His words reflected a deep reverence for Jesus and a clear recognition of God's grand purpose. By likening himself to an unworthy servant in relation to Jesus, John set a timeless example of selflessness and true humility.

Moses also exemplified humility. When Eldad and Medad began prophesying in the camp, Joshua suggested stopping them. However, Moses' humility allowed him to rejoice in others' blessings rather than feeling threatened, showing that true humility fosters unity and contentment.

When Moses faced jealousy and rivalry, he did not react with anger or defensiveness. Instead, he demonstrated patience, relying on God to address their envy (Numbers 12:1-15). His strategy was clear: maintain humility and trust in God's justice rather than engaging in conflict. This approach can help us rise above jealousy without allowing it to disturb our peace.

Hannah's humility remained unwavering, even after the fulfillment of her long-desired blessing. Her prayer in 1 Samuel 2:1-10 is filled with gratitude and praise for God rather than self-exaltation. By acknowledging that *"There is no one holy like Jehovah,"* she demonstrated her humble recognition of God's sovereignty and active role in her life.

4. Respect For God's Arrangement

John the Baptist respected the role that God had assigned to Jesus. He redirected the concerns his disciples had about Jesus' growing following by saying, *"That one must keep on increasing, but I must keep on decreasing"* (John 3:30). By respecting Jesus' role, John demonstrated that acknowledging God's arrangement fosters peace and unity.

John's strategy was to anchor his identity in his God-given role rather than comparing his influence to that of Jesus. By recognizing that all blessings and roles are part of God's arrangement, we can avoid the trap of comparison and embrace fulfillment with our unique purpose.

Moses demonstrated trust in God's arrangement by wholeheartedly rejoicing when Eldad and Medad were empowered to serve, even though they were not formally among the seventy elders gathered at the tent of meeting. Rather than viewing their actions as a challenge, Moses embraced their participation as evidence of God's spirit at work. His reaction reflected his unwavering confidence that God could use anyone He chose to fulfill His purpose. This perspective underscored Moses's deep trust that the work of leading and guiding the people ultimately belonged to God, not to any individual.

Like Abraham, who was willing to offer Isaac in obedience to God, Hannah's trust in God's arrangement is demonstrated by her willingness to dedicate Samuel to His service. She prioritized God's will and honored her vow without hesitation, stating, "I, in turn, now lend him to Jehovah. For all his days, he is lent to Jehovah" (1 Samuel 1:28). This act reflected her confidence in God's arrangement, trusting that Samuel's life would be used for a greater purpose in God's service. By surrendering what she held most dear, Hannah demonstrated a deep understanding of God's sovereignty and wisdom in directing the lives of His servants.

5. Contentment

Even at the height of his popularity, John demonstrated remarkable contentment by refusing to seek personal acclaim for his success. When questioned about his identity, he confidently and humbly identified himself as "a voice of someone crying out in the wilderness, 'Make the way of Jehovah straight'" (John 1:23). This response reflected his deep satisfaction with his role. By finding fulfillment in glorifying

God and supporting others, John exemplified the peace and joy that come from focusing on God's will above all else.

Hannah found contentment in trusting God's timing. Despite years of childlessness, she did not allow bitterness or envy to consume her. Hannah kept her vow and returned her son to serve at the tabernacle. In her prayer of gratitude, she declared, "My heart rejoices in Jehovah; My horn is exalted by Jehovah. My mouth is opened wide against my enemies, for I rejoice in your acts of salvation" (1 Samuel 2:1). Her prayer reflects her deep gratitude.

Moses' contentment is strikingly evident in his decision to abandon the status and comforts of Egyptian royalty to pursue God's calling. Rather than clinging to a life of luxury and power, he humbly embraced the role of a shepherd in Midian, which was a significant change. Hebrews 11:24-25 highlights his decision: "By faith Moses, when grown up, refused to be called the son of Pharaoh's daughter, choosing to be mistreated with the people of God rather than to have the temporary enjoyment of sin."

Moses' willingness to prioritize God's purpose over personal comfort exemplifies the strength that comes from contentment rooted in faith. His example teaches us that true satisfaction comes not from status or possessions but from wholeheartedly embracing our role in God's arrangement, no matter how humble it may appear.

Cultivating Qualities That Rise Above Jealousy

The examples of John the Baptist, Moses, and Hannah illustrate that avoiding jealousy is possible. These faithful individuals cultivated qualities that enabled them to trust in God's arrangement and find peace amidst challenging circumstances.

John found fulfillment in recognizing that all blessings come from God, which helped him embrace his unique role without making comparisons. Moses relied on patience and unwavering trust in God to navigate criticism and jealousy, maintaining his integrity even when challenged by those closest to him.

Hannah demonstrated a heart full of gratitude, focusing on God's blessings and dedicating her gifts to His service rather than harboring bitterness.

These examples remind us that avoiding jealousy requires active effort in exercising strong faith, genuine love, humility, respect for God's arrangement, and contentment. By reflecting on these qualities, we can safeguard our relationships and deepen our bond with God.

When we cultivate these qualities, we transform moments of envy into opportunities for spiritual growth. Truly, avoiding jealousy is not just about what we don't feel—it's about what we actively nurture. As we strive to reflect these qualities, we align ourselves more closely with God's purpose, creating a life characterized by peace, joy, and spiritual harmony.

Chapter 13: The Origin Of Jealousy

In Chapter 3, we explored the tragic account of Abel and the deadly consequences of his brother Cain's jealousy. However, the origins of jealousy extend far beyond the events involving these two siblings. To truly understand this destructive emotion, we must journey back even further—to a time before the events of Cain and Abel—when jealousy first took root in the heart of one of God's spirit creatures.

> *"The past is never dead. It's not even past."* —William Faulkner

You might wonder why examining this early origin is necessary. Faulkner's words suggest that understanding the root of a problem empowers us to address its ongoing influence. Jealousy, like other negative emotions, continues to corrupt hearts and relationships. By exploring its genesis, we can better comprehend its dangers and find the motivation to reject it entirely. Distancing ourselves from jealousy aligns us with a spirit of peace rather than rebellion. This choice becomes more than an act of self-improvement; it is also a stand against its source—the very embodiment of jealousy and every other harmful emotion.

The Bible warns us about the devastating effects of jealousy, emphasizing how this emotion leads to many bad things:

> *"But if you have bitter jealousy and contentiousness in your hearts, do not be bragging and lying against the truth. This is not the wisdom that comes down from above; it is earthly, animalistic, demonic. For wherever there are jealousy and contentiousness, there will also be disorder and every vile thing."* —James 3:14-16

Before Satan became a rebel, he was a trusted angel with an honored position in heaven. However, he allowed envy to take root in his heart, which ultimately ignited negative emotions.

Satan craved the honor and worship that rightfully belonged to Jehovah alone. When Adam and Eve were created, instead of rejoicing in their unique relationship with God, Satan's jealousy drove him to undermine their trust in Jehovah. He deceived Eve, leading both her and Adam into rebellion against God.

This origin story reveals the essence of jealousy: dissatisfaction with one's position and a desire for what belongs to another. Reflecting on this initial case helps us identify how this pattern —craving what others have, which leads to harm—repeats throughout history. Satan's jealousy led to catastrophic consequences, not only for himself but for all of humanity. For this reason, James 3:15 highlights that jealousy is demonic.

The book of Isaiah captures the ambition of the King of Babylon, whose pride and arrogance mirrored Satan's spirit of rebellion. It states:

> "You said in your heart, 'I will ascend to the heavens. Above the stars of God I will lift up my throne, and I will sit down on the mountain of meeting, in the remotest parts of the north. I will go up above the tops of the clouds; I will make myself resemble the Most High.'" —Isaiah 14:13-14

Although primarily directed at the Babylonian dynasty, these words symbolically describe Satan himself. Satan's twisted ambition to rival God fueled this attitude, disrupting God's arrangement. This selfish desire severed Satan's relationship with God, disrupted the harmony in heaven, and introduced death into the world.

By learning to distance ourselves from jealousy, we align ourselves with God and reject the spirit of rebellion that Satan exemplifies. Such a stance safeguards our hearts, strengthens our relationships, and brings us closer to the peace and happiness that Jehovah desires for us.

Jealousy And Pride—An Explosive Combination

As jealousy gives rise to pride, it often intertwines with negative thoughts, creating a potent cycle that erodes relationships, fosters rivalry, and distances us from God. To break free, we must recognize how these elements feed into one another, exasperating the situation.

To understand how these emotions work together, it is helpful to think of them as a fire. Just as a fire requires three elements —a spark to ignite it, fuel to sustain it, and oxygen to keep it alive—jealousy, negative thoughts, and pride, each plays a crucial role in this explosive cocktail. If jealousy acts as the spark, then negative thoughts and pride keep the fire burning, consuming and destroying everything in its path. This inferno severed Satan's relationship with God and introduced sin and suffering into the world. The destructive consequences of this fire have endured throughout history, leaving humanity to grapple with its devastating effects.

Over the centuries, this blaze has proven impossible to extinguish, continuing to burn and leaving ruins in its wake. From broken relationships to shattered trust, jealousy's impact remains as destructive now as it was back in Eden. By examining the interplay between jealousy, negative thinking, and pride, we can better understand their destructive potential and take decisive steps to distance ourselves from their harmful influences.

Jealousy: The Spark That Ignites Pride

Pride comes before a fall. In like manner, jealousy comes before pride, acting as the spark that ignites the entire destructive cycle. Cain's jealousy gave rise to pride, which fueled his resentment and ultimately drove him to commit murder. When encouraged by prideful thoughts and insecurities, jealousy can lead to actions that harm others deeply. The longer we allow jealousy to fester, the more it consumes us, like an unrelenting fire.

The account of the Pharisees and chief priests during Jesus' ministry demonstrates how jealousy can lead to destructive actions. As Jesus gained followers and performed miracles, his teachings exposed the hypocrisy and self-righteousness of the religious leaders. Instead of rejoicing in the good being done and recognizing him as the Messiah, they allowed jealousy to take root. Their envy blinded them to God's purpose, leading them to plot against Jesus and ultimately seek his death. Matthew 27:18 states that *"Pilate was aware that out of envy they had handed him over."* Like a consuming fire, their jealousy destroyed their peace and drove them to oppose God's will.

In our lives, jealousy can lead to similarly destructive patterns. It may manifest as harmful gossip, resentment, or actions meant to undermine others. These behaviors hurt others and damage our spiritual standing. To extinguish jealousy, we must stop feeding it. This requires a deliberate shift in focus—from what others have to what Jehovah has lovingly provided.

Philippians 4:11-12 encourages contentment:

> *"I have learned to be self-sufficient regardless of my circumstances. I know how to be low on provisions and how to have an abundance." —Philippians 4:11-12*

By cultivating an attitude of gratitude, we deprive jealousy of its power, allowing peace, unity, and joy to thrive. This practice helps protect our relationships, strengthens our faith, and demonstrates our love for God and those we hold dear. At the same time, we take a firm stand against Satan and his attempts to exploit this harmful emotion.

Negative Thoughts: The Fuel That Feeds The Fire

Negative thoughts—such as self-pity, suspicion, and resentment—perpetuate the cycle of destruction. They serve as the fuel that feeds jealousy's fire, creating an environment in which it can grow and thrive unchecked.

Negative thinking often starts subtly, feeding on comparisons, insecurities, and dissatisfaction. For instance, thoughts like "Why him and not me?" or "I deserve better" reflect a mindset that breathes life into jealousy. These internal dialogues reinforce feelings of entitlement or inadequacy, creating fertile ground for destructive emotions to thrive. Instead of focusing on our blessings or trusting in God's arrangement, negative thoughts magnify perceived injustices.

This was evident in the case of Jesus. Despite his miraculous works, profound teachings, and compassion, the religious leaders grew increasingly envious of him. They reasoned among themselves, saying: *"If we let him go on this way, they will all put faith in him, and the Romans will come and take away both our place and our nation"* (John 11:48). Their jealousy and fear of losing authority led them to conspire, with Caiaphas declaring, *"it is [better] for one man to die in behalf of the people rather than for the whole nation to be destroyed"* (John 11:50).

Instead of acknowledging the blessings and guidance Jesus brought, the religious leaders allowed their jealousy to fester, twisting their thoughts into a plot to have Jesus killed. This example illustrates the dangers of jealousy fueled by negative thinking and self-interest. It reminds us of the importance of focusing on humility and trust in Jehovah's arrangement to avoid similar pitfalls.

Our negative thinking feeds jealousy and creates an atmosphere in which these emotions thrive. Dwelling on comparisons, harboring grudges, or constantly seeking validation from others gives rise to dissatisfaction and blinds us to God's blessings. Over time, this pattern of thought fuels the flames of envy and becomes a self-perpetuating cycle, making it increasingly difficult to break free from envy's grip.

Breaking this cycle requires a deliberate effort to deprive envy of the fuel it needs to thrive. The Bible encourages us to focus on positive, uplifting thoughts that align with Jehovah's purpose:

> *"[...]Whatever things are true, whatever things are of serious concern, whatever things are righteous, whatever things are chaste, whatever things are lovable, whatever things are well-spoken-of, whatever things are virtuous, and whatever things are praiseworthy, continue considering these things."* —Philippians 4:8

Recognizing that our negative thoughts feed the fire of jealousy is a crucial step in extinguishing these destructive emotions. By taking control of our thoughts and aligning them with God's principles, we starve the fire of jealousy, replacing it with peace and a sense of fulfillment. This, in turn, creates an environment where love, unity, and gratitude can flourish, leaving no room for the destructive flames of envy.

Pride: Oxygen That Sustains The Blaze

For a fire to continue burning, it needs oxygen—the element that keeps the flames alive and intensifies the heat. This is the role of pride, as it often amplifies negative emotions. Pride can prevent us from recognizing our mistakes or being humble, thereby prolonging conflict and strife. By letting go of pride, we can often extinguish these negative feelings.

Pride can block us from seeing our own jealousy, prevent self-reflection, and lead us to blame others. Instead of examining our own thoughts and feelings, pride convinces us that the problem lies with others—their actions, their success, or their perceived advantages. This refusal to acknowledge our own flawed thinking creates a barrier to self-awareness, making it easier to justify jealousy while overlooking its destructive roots. As a result, pride blinds us to the need for change and perpetuates the cycle of jealousy.

The actions of the religious leaders of Jesus' day were deeply rooted in their pride over their heritage and traditions. They prided themselves on being descendants of Abraham and on their strict adherence to the Law and oral traditions. This pride created a barrier that prevented them from seeing the fulfillment of God's promises through Jesus. In John 8:33, when Jesus spoke of setting people free, they replied, *"We are Abraham's offspring and never have been slaves to anyone. How is it you say, 'You will become free'?"* Their boast about their lineage and traditions made them resistant to Jesus' message of spiritual freedom and humility.

By clinging to their self-righteousness, the religious leaders allowed pride to reinforce their jealousy, further hardening their hearts against God's purpose. Their pride in tradition and heritage blinded them to the deeper spiritual truths Jesus taught and to their own need for repentance. This teaches us to avoid letting pride in what we achieve or where we come from stop our spiritual growth and acceptance of Jehovah's guidance. Humility, rather than pride, allows us to stay aligned with God's will.

Pride inflates our sense of self-worth and entitlement, making us overly focused on ourselves and what we believe we deserve. For example, Satan's pride blinded him to the wrongfulness of his ambitions. Instead of humbly recognizing God's rightful sovereignty, Satan twisted the situation to portray God as withholding something from others. His inability to reflect on his motives led him to deceive Eve and drag humanity into rebellion. Similarly, when pride dominates our thinking, it prevents us from seeing the role our mindsets play in fostering jealousy, making it much harder to address and correct.

God's Word provides a powerful antidote to pride. Proverbs 16:18 warns:

> "Pride is before a crash, and a haughty spirit before stumbling." —Proverbs 16:18

This advice reminds us that pride can be harmful and encourages us to be humble, which honors God and promotes unity. By being humble and letting God's principles guide our thoughts, we disempower pride, encourage honest self-reflection, and protect our hearts.

Breaking The Cycle

Having explored the destructive interplay between jealousy, negative thoughts, and pride, let's now focus on actionable steps. What practical tools can help us extinguish this blaze and restore harmony to our lives?

The events in Eden underscore the need to guard our hearts against jealousy. By cultivating humility, contentment, and loyalty to God, we can resist the intoxicating flames of jealousy and avoid the devastation it brings. These qualities allow us to maintain balance in our relationships and foster a close bond with our Creator, shielding us from the destructive cycle that began with Satan's rebellion.

Breaking the cycle of jealousy ultimately means distancing ourselves from Satan and his influence. Jealousy's origin in Satan's rebellion highlights its deeply harmful nature and its capacity to sever our relationship with Jehovah. When we reject jealousy, we safeguard our spiritual health and take a stand against the very traits that define Satan. By doing so, we align ourselves with God's wisdom.

James 4:7 encourages us to resist Satan's influence, stating:

> "Subject yourselves to God; but oppose the Devil, and he will flee from you." —James 4:7

Actively distancing ourselves from jealousy requires a conscious effort to recognize its destructive potential and its origin in rebellion. This involves examining our thoughts, motives, and actions to ensure they reflect humility and contentment. By cultivating gratitude for God's blessings and seeking to imitate His loving qualities, we starve jealousy of its power and weaken Satan's grip on our lives.

Taking this stand also deepens our trust in Jehovah. Instead of comparing ourselves to others or coveting what they have, we focus on what truly matters—our relationship with God and the spiritual blessings He provides. This shift in perspective transforms our hearts, allowing us to experience the joy and peace that come from living in harmony with His principles.

In distancing ourselves from jealousy and its source, we become beacons of light in a world marred by envy. Our example can inspire others to break free from the cycle of jealousy and turn toward the peace and unity that only God can provide. This proactive approach strengthens our faith while also reinforcing our commitment.

Chapter 14: Conclusion

T hroughout this book, we have explored how jealousy, as a powerful emotion, can disrupt relationships, harm personal well-being, and disturb inner peace. By understanding the origins of jealousy, we recognize that yielding to its seductive allure renders us subservient to its true source, Satan, the father of jealousy. This recognition is essential because jealousy is not merely an emotion; it is a destructive force that can distort our perception of others and ourselves. It thrives on comparison, fosters resentment, and erodes relationships. When we succumb to jealousy, we allow it to influence our actions and decisions, often leading to harmful consequences. This surrender can create a cycle of bitterness and dissatisfaction, distancing us from family, friends, and God.

Satan embodies deceit and discord. His role as the originator of jealousy is exemplified in his fall from grace, driven by envy of God's authority and glory. By giving in to jealousy, we echo that same rebellion, prioritizing selfish desires over the harmony and well-being of our relationships and spiritual health. This makes us unwitting participants in a narrative of destruction that stands in opposition to the principles of faith, humility, and selflessness.

Recognizing jealousy as a tool of Satan underscores the importance of resisting its influence. Instead of succumbing to envy, we are called to cultivate virtues that counteract its power: contentment with what we have, celebration of others' successes, and trust in our God. By doing so, we break free from the chains of jealousy and align ourselves with a path of peace and spiritual growth. In this way, understanding the origins of jealousy becomes not just an act of awareness but a powerful step toward liberation and alignment with Jehovah's principles.

"Strive not to be a success, but rather to be of value." — Albert Einstein

Jealousy, at its core, often arises from a misunderstanding of success. In a world that frequently measures success through material gains, recognition, or achievements, it is easy to feel inadequate when we compare ourselves to others. However, true success is not defined by surpassing others but by faith, humility, and alignment with a higher purpose.

Abel, whose genuine devotion to God earned His favor. Joseph, despite enduring severe trials, remained steadfast in his faith and ultimately rose to a position where he could save countless lives. Similarly, David faced immense opposition but achieved lasting success because he trusted in God. These individuals remind us that real success lies in fully realizing the opportunities entrusted to us and using them to bring honor to God, not in competing with or outperforming others.

The irony of success is that it often inspires both admiration and envy. While a blessing, success can become a battleground when it provokes jealousy in others. Biblical accounts, such as those of Cain and Saul, illustrate this tension. These stories show how envy can corrode relationships and lead to devastating outcomes.

Yet, the effects of jealousy are not irreversible. By learning from these biblical examples and applying God's wisdom, we can defeat envy. Instead of allowing jealousy to consume us, we can cultivate contentment and gratitude. This shift transforms jealousy's destructive energy into an opportunity for growth and fosters reconciliation.

Commit To Take Action

Having examined the sources of jealousy and the destructive interplay between pride, jealousy, and negative thoughts in Chapter 13, let us now review the actionable steps provided in this book. What practical tools can we use to extinguish the blaze of envy and restore harmony to our lives?

Helping Others

Chapter 5 outlined steps we can take to avoid provoking jealousy in others, emphasizing humility, generosity, and collaboration. However, you might wonder: Why should I be responsible for addressing a situation when someone else is harboring jealousy toward me? Shouldn't they be accountable for their own emotions and actions?

While this concern is understandable, such questions often adopt a narrow focus and overlook the broader goal of fostering peace and harmony. We are called to be peacemakers and to promote unity in our relationships. Romans 12:18 reminds us, "*If possible, as far as it depends on you, be peaceable with all men.*"

Moreover, taking proactive steps to avoid provoking jealousy demonstrates a spirit of selflessness and empathy. It reflects our desire to prioritize the well-being of others over the defense of our rights. This does not mean excusing harmful behavior or bearing undue blame, but rather fostering an environment where jealousy has less opportunity to thrive. In this way, we deprive the fire of jealousy of oxygen, giving it no room to grow. As a result, our conduct becomes a powerful witness, inspiring others to reflect on their own feelings and attitudes.

While we cannot control how others feel or act, we can take steps to ensure that our actions do not intentionally or inadvertently contribute to discord. To help remember the strategies from Chapter 5, consider using the acronym SHARE as outlined below. By applying this model, we can actively foster environments where collaboration, generosity, and mutual respect flourish. These actions promote positive relationships and help minimize the potential for envy.

1. S - *Share Generously*: Share resources, time, and support with others to foster unity and reduce feelings of competition.

2. H - *Humility*: Avoid boasting about accomplishments. Instead, highlight others' contributions and successes in conversations.

3. A - *Acknowledge Others' Contributions*: Publicly recognize the efforts and achievements of others, whether in personal or professional settings.

4. R - *Respect in Sharing*: Before sharing your successes, consider how your words may affect others' feelings, especially during their challenges.

5. E - *Encourage Teamwork Over Competition*: Invite others to participate in your projects or goals, emphasizing teamwork and shared success rather than rivalry.

Proactively addressing jealousy can yield significant long-term benefits. Relationships plagued by unresolved jealousy often fester, leading to tension and distrust that hinder cooperation and disrupt personal peace. By taking the initiative to de-escalate such situations, we prevent future conflicts and lay the foundation for stronger, more harmonious connections. In essence, the effort we invest in nurturing relationships today contributes to our peace and joy in the future. Over time, the goodwill cultivated through addressing jealousy with wisdom and grace can foster deeper trust, mutual respect, and even meaningful collaboration with those who may have once harbored envy.

Helping Yourself

Chapter 6 focused on strategies to overcome jealousy within ourselves, emphasizing introspection, gratitude, and reliance on God's guidance. As in the preceding section, you might ask, "Why should I make such an effort to address my own jealousy? Isn't it a natural emotion that everyone experiences?"

While jealousy is indeed a common human response, allowing it to fester compromises our relationships, clouds our judgment, and damages our spiritual health. Overcoming it involves cultivating a heart that aligns with Jehovah's qualities of love and peace.

We cannot control the thoughts, feelings, and actions of others, but we have the power to control our own. This realization is both empowering and liberating. Instead of being trapped by the emotional turmoil that jealousy creates, we can take ownership of our responses and actively choose a path of growth and contentment. By doing so, we free ourselves from jealousy's grip and open the door to greater peace and spiritual strength. There is a freedom that comes from knowing that our emotional well-being does not depend on how others act or what they achieve; rather, it is shaped by our relationship with God.

The practical steps outlined in Chapter 6 are designed to help us uproot jealousy and replace it with contentment. To easily recall these strategies, consider using the acronym PEACE, as outlined below. The PEACE framework provides a practical and spiritually enriching pathway to free ourselves from jealousy's grip and cultivate a life filled with peace, joy, and spiritual growth. By applying these actions, we can view the successes of others not as threats but as opportunities to celebrate God's blessings.

1. P - *Pray to Jehovah*: Use prayer and meditation to request help in replacing envy with contentment and peace.

2. E - *Examine Your Motives*: Regularly ask yourself why you feel envious and identify whether it stems from unmet desires or comparisons.

3. A - *Appreciate Your Blessings*: Make a daily habit of listing specific things for which you are thankful, shifting your focus from what you lack to what you have.

4. C - *Concentrate on Your Responsibilities*: Concentrate on excelling in your current roles and tasks rather than fixating on what others are doing.

5. E - *Eliminate Comparisons*: Focus on your unique journey by reflecting on your personal goals and strengths instead of comparing yourself to others.

By taking these steps, we extinguish jealousy at its source and reflect the love and peace that God desires for all His servants. This journey is not just about improving ourselves; it is about finding joy and freedom in living a life that contributes to liberating others.

Imitate Desirable Traits

Chapter 12 highlights key traits that empower us to rise above jealousy and reflect Jehovah's qualities in our lives. The practical strategies in Chapters 5 and 6 can help us manage jealousy, but the cultivating traits discussed in Chapter 12 go deeper. These qualities transform our responses to jealousy and our entire outlook on life.

The difference between strategies and traits is similar to the difference between *doing* and *being*. Strategies guide our actions in specific situations, helping us address jealousy in the moment. Traits, on the other hand, shape who we are at our core, influencing how we naturally respond to challenges over time. By embedding these traits into our character, we create a foundation of strength and resilience, ensuring that jealousy has less opportunity to take hold from the outset.

Focusing on these traits shifts the power dynamic. Instead of reacting to external circumstances or comparisons, we proactively align our hearts with God's character.

1. *Strong Faith*: Trust that God's timing and arrangements are perfect for your needs, even if blessings seem delayed.

2. *Genuine Love*: Make it a priority to wholeheartedly celebrate others' successes, knowing that it strengthens your relationships.

3. *Humility*: Acknowledge that all blessings come from God, fostering a mindset of gratitude and modesty.

4. *Respect for God's Arrangement*: Remind yourself that everyone has a unique role and path assigned by Jehovah, and trust in His justice.

5. *Contentment*: Focus on the peace and satisfaction that come from appreciating God's provisions in your life.

When these traits become a part of our character, they act as a protective shield, enabling us to reflect God's love and peace in all aspects of our lives. By nurturing these qualities, we create a life that is harmonious, fulfilling, and deeply aligned with God's purpose for us.

Humility—A Strategy And Trait

Humility serves as both a strategy and a character trait, highlighting its multifaceted role in our lives. This unique quality operates much like a superpower, influencing how we navigate specific situations. As a strategy, humility guides our actions by encouraging us to minimize personal achievements, recognize others' contributions, and avoid behaviors that might provoke jealousy. As a character trait, it forms the foundation of our personality, shaping how we see ourselves, others, and Jehovah. This dual role makes humility an essential quality for fostering peace and unity.

In many ways, humility is similar to the quality of love, which should run like a golden thread through all our interactions and relationships. Just as love enables us to prioritize others and reflect God's qualities, humility teaches us to approach every relationship with modesty and selflessness. It is a quality that softens pride, tempers jealousy, and creates space for compassion and understanding. When humility is present, we are less likely to see others as rivals and more likely to appreciate their unique gifts and contributions.

Humility also has a compounding effect. It impacts our actions *and* influences how others perceive and respond to us. A humble person inspires trust, diffuses conflict, and fosters collaboration. By prioritizing humility, we signal to others that we value relationships over recognition and unity over competition. Much like love, humility acts as a bridge that connects us to Jehovah's purpose, helping us reflect His qualities in a way that draws others closer to Him.

Like love, humility is not a one-time choice but a continual effort to align our hearts with God's. When humility becomes a defining aspect of who we are, it transforms our relationships with others and our relationship with Jehovah, allowing us to experience deeper peace, joy, and fulfillment.

Grow In Love

Implementing the ten strategies outlined in Chapters 5 and 6, along with cultivating the five traits in Chapter 12, may initially feel overwhelming. However, taking it step by step—such as focusing on one element per month—can make the process feel more manageable. This gradual approach aligns with the wisdom of the following proverb:

> *"Be not afraid of growing slowly; be afraid only of standing still."* —Chinese Proverb

Meaningful transformation often requires patience and persistence. By progressing steadily, you allow each element to take root and become a natural part of how you approach relationships.

Rather than being discouraged by the pace of change, embracing incremental growth ensures that the adjustments are lasting and impactful. Over time, this deliberate effort enables you to effectively transform toxic relationships marred by envy. The cumulative effect of these small, consistent steps can foster healthier interactions, build trust, and replace envy with mutual respect and understanding. Remember, progress—no matter how slow—is far more valuable than remaining stagnant.

> *"On these two commandments the whole Law hangs, and the Prophets."* —Matthew 22:40

The phrase *"the whole Law"* that Jesus mentioned in Matthew 22:40 refers to the Torah, the first five books of the Bible that contain the Mosaic Law, while *"the Prophets"* represents the teachings and writings of the prophets, which offer guidance, correction, and elaboration on God's will. Together, *"the Law and the Prophets"* serve as a synecdoche that encapsulates the entirety of Jewish Scripture.

Through this statement, Jesus was summarizing the essence of God's commandments and teachings as found in the Hebrew Scriptures. The question then arises: On which two commandments do the Law and the Prophets hang? The answer is found in the three verses preceding verse 40:

> "[...] You must love Jehovah your God with your whole heart and with your whole soul and with your whole mind. This is the greatest and first commandment. The second, like it, is this: You must love your neighbor as yourself." — Matthew 22:37-39

These two commandments form the foundation of all other laws and teachings. Loving God wholeheartedly encompasses devotion, worship, and obedience, while loving one's neighbor entails compassion, justice, and kindness in relationships.

In reality, the strategies outlined in Chapters 5 and 6 are valuable tools, but they can be simplified into the timeless principles found in Matthew 22:37-39. To truly uproot envy from our hearts, we need only apply these two commandments: love God with all our heart, soul, and mind, and love our neighbor as ourselves. These verses encompass the essence of every strategy for addressing envy, as they direct our focus toward wholehearted devotion to God and genuine care for others. When we align our thoughts and actions with these guiding principles, envy naturally diminishes, and our relationships transform into reflections of God's love. The path to overcoming envy does not require complexity but rather a sincere commitment to living out these foundational principles.

Love is the antidote. But what does it mean to love? The essence of love is beautifully described in 1 Corinthians 13:4-7, where love is defined by its qualities:

> "Love is patient and kind. Love is not jealous. It does not brag, does not get puffed up, does not behave indecently, does not look for its own interests, does not become provoked. It does not keep account of the injury. It does not rejoice over unrighteousness, but rejoices with the truth. It bears all things, believes all things, hopes all things, endures all things." —1 Corinthians 13:4-7

These verses offer a practical blueprint for understanding love as an active choice rather than a fleeting emotion. True love requires effort; it involves putting the needs of others above our own, remaining calm under provocation, and forgiving generously.

When we examine envy through the lens of this type of love, we see how incompatible the two are. Envy thrives on comparison, self-interest, and resentment, all of which are the opposite of love's unselfish and self-sacrificing nature. By cultivating patience, kindness, and a willingness to rejoice in others' success, we strip envy of its power. Love transforms our perspective, enabling us to celebrate the gifts and achievements of others as extensions of God's abundant kindness. Love, in its truest form, is the cure to envy.

A Journey To Peace

Finally, we must remember that jealousy was never part of Jehovah's original purpose. It is a perversion introduced by Satan, and as such, it is an emotion we can overcome. While this may seem challenging or even impossible, Jesus reassures us in Matthew 19:26: "*With men this is impossible, but with God all things are possible.*" By relying on God's help and rejecting the comparison and competition that fuel jealousy, we can cultivate a mindset rooted in unity, peace, and mutual encouragement.

The journey to overcoming jealousy and finding peace is not without challenges, but it is one filled with life-changing rewards. As highlighted in the introduction of this book, you *can* lead a life free from the burden of comparison, where you celebrate the successes of others as sincerely as you celebrate your own—a life where relationships are marked by trust, love, and collaboration rather than rivalry and contention. This is the life God desires for you—a life of unity, joy, and abundance.

As we move forward, let us take the lessons from this exploration to heart. When faced with feelings of jealousy, we can pause, reflect, and turn to God for help. Let us cultivate thankfulness for our unique blessings and strive to build others up, as reminded in 1 Thessalonians 5:11, which says: "*Therefore, keep encouraging one another and building one another up, just as you are in fact doing.*"

Most importantly, let us continue to trust in God's wisdom and timing. He ultimately knows what is best for us and *when* it is best for us. Trusting in His plans allows us to let go of envy and to rest in the assurance that He will provide for our needs. Jeremiah 29:11 reminds us of His loving intentions:

> "'For I well know the thoughts that I am thinking toward you,' declares Jehovah, 'thoughts of peace, and not of calamity, to give you a future and a hope." —Jeremiah 29:11

May your journey toward peace and happiness draw you closer to Jehovah. By embracing humility, love, and contentment, you can transform jealousy into a stepping stone to freedom.

THE END